Philosophy Sketches

700 Words at a Time

Alexander E. Hooke

Apprentice House Press

Loyola University Maryland

Cover photo: "Organ Grinder at the local Harvest Festival," by Kathy, October 20, 2007; licensed under the Creative Commons Attribution 2.0 Generic license.

First Edition

Paperback ISBN: 978-1-62720-172-8
Ebook ISBN: 978-1-62720-173-5

Printed in the United States of America

Design: Ellen Roussel
Marketing: Ryan McNulty

Published by Apprentice House

Apprentice
House Press
Loyola University Maryland

Apprentice House
Loyola University Maryland
4501 N. Charles Street
Baltimore, MD 21210
410.617.5265 • 410.617.2198 (fax)
www.ApprenticeHouse.com
info@ApprenticeHouse.com

Philosophy Sketches

700 Words at a Time

For Erika and Nicky

The Child is innocence and forgetfulness, a new beginning, a sport, a self-propelling wheel, a first motion, a sacred Yes.
—Nietzsche

Contents

Preface

Philosophy embraces a variety of venues to help develop and convey our thoughts and ideas. Dialogues, confessions, arguments, meditations, articles, treatises, aphorisms, and critiques are among the most prevalent. The essay has also been a frequent venue.

Several features distinguish the essay. It avoids technical language and scholarly citations. It usually focuses on a single theme without requiring extensive background knowledge from the reader. Unlike a structured and detailed argument, an essay can be somewhat freewheeling, interweaving personal anecdotes while incorporating other fields of knowledge. Finally, whereas it can take days or weeks to read a lengthy scholarly article or book, an essay needs only one sitting.

With the emergence of the newspaper as part of everyday life in the 1800s, the essay has assumed a special place for commenting on human affairs—namely, the op-ed page. The term refers to "opposite the editorial page." Editorials generally reflect the views and attitudes of a newspaper's basic principles and positions. The op-ed page presents contrary views, independent voices, well known writers as well as relatively anonymous figures. Amid this variety, there is one basic guideline for an op-ed essay: it should be about 700 words.

As a journalist-wanna-be, I've always enjoyed the newspaper. In my early teens I was a paperboy for three years, then a sports writer or editor-in-chief for two college papers. Between graduate schools I also worked as an assistant editor and chief reporter for a Baltimore monthly, then an advertisement messenger for the major daily. When visiting a metropolis or small town, one of the first things I do is buy the local paper. Reading news items and commentaries offers a glimpse into the everyday controversies and disputes demanding the attention of the town's residents and civic leaders.

Over the years I have tried to bring a philosophical focus to current issues by contributing essays to local newspapers, mostly *The Baltimore Sun*. People often assume that philosophy deals only with abstract and timeless themes. Students required to take a philosophy course understandably share this assumption when their textbooks bear overwhelming titles such as "Twenty Great Truths" or "The Enduring Questions." This is misleading. Most philosophers have been quite attuned to ordinary events and struggles. Be it war, political leadership, injustice, religious quarrels, uncertain advances in science, human aspirations and frailties, death, ordinary virtues and vices, contemporary controversies and issues have always attracted the attention of most thinkers.

Admittedly, a philosophical perspective infrequently resolves a controversy or proposes a satisfactory solution to a current problem. How many perspectives do? Philosophy helps us reconsider our views or see a problem from an unfamiliar angle. Sometimes it can approach a topic with more intensity or with some levity. Many of the following essays have drawn few comments. Others sparked numerous rejoinders, some very thoughtful that made me reconsider my own points and others that left me wondering if the respondent actually read the entire essay.

Calling the following essays "sketches" evokes carnival or street artists who draw people's profiles in five minutes or so. Op-ed essays take more than five minutes to write, but they are usually read within five minutes. So the writer tries for conciseness and brevity, unlike the dialogue, treatise or scholarly text that can elaborate on a theme for pages while interweaving arcane asides and footnotes. A philosophy sketch via the op-ed page offers general readers a chance to revisit their thoughts in a way that is inaccessible should they approach an academic forum.

By presenting the essays in this format, I hope readers recognize both the independence of philosophical thought as well as their own efforts in thinking through the controversies and absurdities that have emerged in their lives. At the same time, they are presented with a sense of collage. One is welcome to begin anywhere.

Thanks to the kind folks of nearby locales Sweet 27 and The Dizz for such gracious hospitality. Their music, fire place and tasty refreshments offered me a tranquil retreat to go over these essays when they were works in progress. I am also indebted to editors who have considered my essays and, when accepted (there have been some rejections), always improved them with their proverbial red pen. I also appreciate their allowing me considerable intellectual latitude. They include Alice Cherbonnier of *The Baltimore Chronicle*, and from *The Baltimore Sun*, Richard Gross, Michael Cross-Barnett and Tricia Bishop. My gratitude to Ellen Roussel, Ryan McNulty, and the production crew at Apprentice House.

1
Celebrating Other Lives

Introduction

Socrates' legendary encounter with the Delphic Oracle ushered in a new task for seekers of truth or lovers of wisdom. She directed Socrates and his followers to "Know Thyself." This is not a clear cut task because the target of our concern is uncertain. Is this a call for introspection or meditation? If we want to know about cooking or auto repairs, we consult experts such as chefs or car mechanics.

It is less clear which experts we contact to learn about ourselves. This raises the dilemma of relying on our own self-awareness or consulting others, such as an expert, friend, counselor, or, when very confused, palm readers and interpreters of our horoscopes.

One response to this dilemma is by first acknowledging what we are not. We are not animals, gods, saints or super heroes. We are mere mortals who should not pretend otherwise. At the same time we should recognize our inclinations, talents or potential, and be prepared to see where they might lead us.

For me, sometimes this dilemma is highlighted when seeing others do admirable things, things I could never do. These individuals are not role models insofar as they embody a way of life for us to emulate. In seeing what they do, they evoke something memorable or special, standing on their own as exemplars of human possibilities. Many are relatively anonymous, some quite well known.

When asked who you admire, the usual responses are a parent, relative, teacher, or friend. They are the ones we know and are close to. Here are sketches of those admired from a distance. I know little about their personal lives, whether they are kind or cruel to their pets, responsible or neglectful parents, contributors to or corrupters of the common good. But in their own distinct way, each contributed some joy or insight to other people's lives. The essays here attempt to convey this joy or insight.

The Essays

Though we share the title of educators, I believe grade school teachers have much greater pedagogical responsibility than I do. When my daughter was ready for pre-K, she went to a nearby Baltimore City public school. Despite the usual cautions about city schools, we gave it a try. We were completely surprised by the everyday energy and good cheer of her teacher Joyce Rosen and assistant Mary Smith. They invariably encouraged and brightened the school days of first year students. Unfortunately, next year was quite the opposite and took a precarious direction, so my daughter did not return to public schools until the 9th grade.

Johns Hopkins University has hosted an annual Spring Fair weekend since the late 1970s. I've been a regular for over fifteen years, ever since my daughter and son were old enough to attend. The Monkey Man, aka Jerry Brown, has always been my favorite. He has a small monkey—friend? collaborator? partner? –with whom he does all sorts of performances. While there are magic tricks, old vaudeville songs, jokes, jocular banter with the crowds, the little guy invariably is the main attraction.

When he gets a momentary break, we talk briefly. He once said that teaching his "Jangko" to be a performer was harder than raising a teenager. When he began appearing at the Spring Fair, fans had cameras but no cell phones. In those days most spectators focused on Brown's performances. Now everyone has a smart phone and the first thing they want is a selfie with the playful primate. With a delightful sense of humor, The Monkey Man's patience and kindness to all sorts of people have endured the technological gadgetry.

I never met Clarence Gaines. His book, *They Call Me Big House,* presents an enlightening portrait of Gaines and twentieth century America. His Baltimore connection is incidental. Upon graduating from Morgan State College, he was hired by Winston-Salem State Teacher's College, in North Carolina. Like Morgan State, it is an HBI, an acronym for "historically black institution." There "Big House" Gaines became the basketball coach and mentor to hundreds of young black Americans for decades.

My connection? He was coach of my boyhood basketball idol—Earl "The Pearl" Monroe, who played four years for the Baltimore Bullets and was one of the most electrifying and inventive figures to ever play the game. In Monroe's senior year, the Winston-Salem Rams had a historic season and won a national championship. (In 2006 I had a full-length article on this team published in *Basketball Times.* I met Monroe and we considered a writing project together, but regrettably things in my personal life prevented me from pursuing it.) More importantly for Coach Gaines, his Monroe-led team was a pinnacle of his unending imperative to have his student-athletes graduate and advance to productive and worthy lives. In this task he had a second imperative—to encourage opportunities of integration in Winston Salem, for which local journalist Mary Garber said he did more than all the politicians put together.

Johns Rawls is ranked among the top twenty philosophers of the twentieth century. *A Theory of Justice,* his major work, sold half a million copies and has been translated into over a dozen languages. This is an unusual accomplishment for a book that is fairly dense reading. Rawls grew up in Baltimore. His two brothers died in their youth, apparently from catching the diseases that had plagued young Rawls. From such tragedy one might understandably conclude that justice is completely arbitrary, a secular version of the axiom, "There but for the grace of God go I." Rawls responded by developing a systematic understanding of the just state by looking into basic tenets of human nature and fundamental principles of fairness.

One summer I took an National Endowment for the Humanities seminar with J.B. Schneewind at Johns Hopkins University. He was a graduate student at Harvard when Rawls defended his dissertation. Students were invited to attend this departmental event. Schneewind recalled how Rawls stunned the audience by quoting to the Harvard professors passages from Kant in the original German. One does not have to be a Rawlsian to find that remarkable.

My college grants me considerable leeway in offering new courses. For one course I wanted to incorporate Grimm's Fairy Tales. I've read to or watched with my two children a number of Grimm's related productions. Somehow I started reading the original tales. They are much different from Disney and children's book versions. More intense and surprising, entertaining but also disturbing—these tales were, simply, more grim. The brothers' version of "Cinderella" concludes with the step-sisters becoming blind from the birds poking out their envious eyes.

The Grimms were primarily linguists setting out to study the historical aspects of the German language. In their research they realized the enduring legacy of folk tales and the many versions in which they were told and retold. The brothers inadvertently paved the wave for later scholarly projects that studied fairy tales or folk stories as universal morality lessons, Freudian struggles with "eros" and "thanatos" (love and death drives), or glimpses into the societies where the tales thrived.

There is a Wednesday in April called "Administrative Assistants Day." This bland euphemism says little about the tasks and responsibilities of those individuals it proposes to respect—secretaries. On this day they receive cards, chocolates, or a bouquet of flowers to be displayed on their desks. Too lazy to get flowers, I thought an essay might do. I had been reading Sissela Bok's *Secrets* where she reviews the etymologies and descriptions related to the secret. This pushed me to consider the careful attention secretaries devote to an endless array of moments and people.

Like the Monkey Man, they are very patient with all types. On occasion people vent their bad moods to secretaries. Secretaries have provided considerable assistance to some of my projects, particularly when they learned and laughed about my technical ineptness. For this essay, I had to obtain permission to use their actual names, since they were not public figures (such as top administrators of colleges and universities). One of them joked, "Yea, well I should be a public figure! I do more than my boss!"

Recognizing John Lennon's 70th birthday risks sentimental idolatry. He was not an ideal husband, he was not an attentive father to his first son Julian, he had a barbed wit, and he got caught up in some odd political causes, such as his bed-in for peace and sending acorns to world leaders. He was also brilliant, generous, focused and immensely curious.

Rock and roll music is, for better or worse, a universal phenomenon and genre of modern art. This can be attributed to the singular accomplishments of The Beatles. The case can be made that Lennon with the Beatles are among the most influential artists of the twentieth century. In a graduate existentialism course I tried to obtain an interview with Lennon while he was hibernating in New York City. I got as far as his lawyer, who said no. Just as well, I would have been a blubbering fool.

This chapter concludes with an appreciation of two collaborators—Carolyn Manuszak and Rose Dawson. Technically, they were my bosses. They were the ones who offered me a full-time position with enough confidence to grant me an intellectual freedom that few people have. Aside from this personal gratitude, Carolyn and Rose contributed to the well-being of generations of college students. For three decades they devoted their efforts to the life and growth of Villa Julie College, often calling each other five or six in the morning to discuss the next day or week's plans and struggles. For their retirement party, I was one of two faculty invited to speak on their behalf. When Carolyn died several years ago, I was again honored to represent the faculty and offer memories of her during a special service.

In Praise of Two Hampden Elementary Teachers

When telling others about our four-year-old daughter attending pre-kindergarten at Hampden Elementary, my wife and I were offered some of the following bits of wisdom. "Did you buy her a gun? She'll need it to defend herself." "A public school? But how will she ever get into an Ivy League college, now?" "She'll be pregnant in ten years."

Apparently we were seen as either ignorant of or indifferent to our child's future. We did not know that the constant fears drummed up by the evening news were to be taken as gospel truth. We did not know that only those pricey private schools guarantee a pre-K child a life of moral virtue and professional success.

But our gloomy prophets and local TV anchors did not know of Ms. Joyce Rosen and her assistant, Mrs. Mary Smith. For thirteen years they have teamed up to teach over 500 of Baltimore's pre-K children. For thirteen years they have greeted each student with a handshake and a "Hello (name), I'm glad you're here today." And they bid each child goodbye with a hug or a sweet treat. Taking a walk along 36th Street, one is astonished how they are stopped by so many young people letting them know how things are going or wishing their former mentors well.

These former students remember how devoted Ms. Rosen and Mrs. Smith were to their own beginnings in education. Patience, encouragement, and attentiveness were some of the virtues these two educators showed in helping Baltimore's four/five-year-olds learn the alphabet, numbers, shapes, rhymes, songs, new words and sounds.

These former students recall how pre-K with Ms. Rosen and Mrs. Smith was not a euphemism for play time. For them pre-K included walks to the Falls Road library, where Miss Vicki would read them stories and sign them up for library cards. For them pre-K meant trips to classical concerts, ventures to the SPCA or zoo, or daily rehearsals of skits and songs which they were to perform for parents in the year-end assembly.

Our daughter has been one of the beneficiaries of this teaching team. Her curiosity, concentration and confidence grew immeasurably during the nine months she spent with them. Her ability to talk and play with others, reenact at home the lessons from school, and identify similarities and difference among things and ideas all reflect a personal and intellectual maturity we could not have anticipated.

No doubt skeptics will remind us about violence in public schools, prospects for Ivy League, and other tidbits from the TV news flashes in order to diminish the enriching experiences of our daughter and the 500-plus other children who have been under the tutelage of Hampden Elementary's Ms. Rosen and Mrs. Smith.

As a teacher myself, I am aware of the uncertain effects one has on students. Yet we need to remind the skeptics of their own ignorance. To educate, as the word's roots indicate, is to "lead out." It is to bring out some of the hidden talents and tap some of the potential strengths every child has.

That our daughter and her classmates learned and discovered so much about themselves and each other in the last year can be attributed only in part to the work of their parents and relatives. Their growth must also be credited to the work of Ms. Joyce Rosen and Mrs. Mary Smith—the educators.

Giving the 'Monkey Man' his due

I propose we set aside an occasional moment to honor those who, outside the limelight of fame and celebrity- hood, are one of a kind. In relative obscurity they contribute something joyful or memorable to our lives in a distinct and singular fashion. For me, Jerry Brown, who's best known as the Monkey Man, is a candidate for this honor.

For two decades The Monkey Man has entertained and enchanted generations of fans throughout the Mid-Atlantic region. With a Capuchin monkey named Django as his sidekick, he has been performing magic tricks, playing music, telling jokes and walking on stilts in carnivals, fairs and schools. Few observers leave his show without a smile or laugh.

Watching him over the years, one cannot help but be impressed by such a talent. In contrast to divas and athletic superstars who perform for two hours before faceless thousands in a darkened arena, the Monkey Man is most often found at carnival grounds for four or five hours entertaining motley individuals face-to-face. His unique blend of energy, intelligence and wit is striking.

Consider his act. Donning top hat, colorful jacket, shoes with dangling bells, and with Django nestled on his shoulder, the Monkey Man strolls through a festival and soon catches the attention of youngsters. Detecting their shyness, he approaches them and smiles. "Is Django friendly?" the kids want to know. "What does the monkey do?" The Monkey Man immediately puts them at ease. He stoops to their eye level, looks right at the child and says, "You are a tree, your arms are branches. Keep still, and Django will sit on you." He must have said this a million times, but each time he tells this to a child, it is as if it is the first time.

Parents can't resist the photo-op of a monkey perched on their child's shoulders, especially if Django also shakes his hand or gives her a quick kiss on the nose. As some college students gather around his act, the Monkey Man switches gears and initiates a discussion with them. He asks if they believe in physical laws of nature or the powers of the mind. Then he shows a steel fork and requests the student to bend the prongs with his fingers. Can't do it. Use your mental powers, prods the Monkey Man. Impossible, says the budding intellectual. With the patter of a magician, the Monkey Man begins bending the fork's prongs without any apparent physical manipulation before the student and a surprised crowd.

He might then bring out an antique accordion or banjo and sing a song or two. He's a veritable walking jukebox. The Monkey Man's repertoire ranges from forlorn love ballads to vaudeville standards. His rendition of "The Monkey in All of Us," a spoof on those riled up about evolution, is a classic. If there is a lull in the action, Jerry Brown patiently answers questions from fans about his work and Django. Time permitting, he relishes telling a joke or two. He talks about the plight of monkeys in various parts of the world, shifts in popular humor and the lasting effects of music. Django is 25 and past middle-age in monkey years. What strikes me most is the energy, enthusiasm and endless curiosity that underscore the Monkey Man's performance. Am I, for example, able to tell students about Plato's Cave Allegory as if it is completely novel to them, even though I talked about it hundreds of times? Jerry Brown has that uncanny ability.

To celebrate being one of kind is to recognize a talent and intelligence that has momentarily made life a bit sweeter. Beyond the world of fame and celebrity, he or she has brought some good cheer to a stranger or passerby. Jerry Brown, the Monkey Man, is my candidate for such an honor. Who's yours?

'Big House' Gaines: His noble way dealt bigotry a beating

"I do not think it matters how disruptive or poor an environment they came from. Every kid can learn." —Clarence E. "Big House" Gaines, 2004

WINSTON-SALEM, N.C., has just buried its most renowned citizen, Clarence "Big House" Gaines. He was its university's basketball coach and athletic director for nearly 50 years. His legacy is such that, according to a local archivist, the funeral marks one of those rare events when Winston-Salem is the center of attention for all of North Carolina. The event deserves the attention of an entire country.

Mr. Gaines was a star football player for Morgan State in the early 1940s. An athletic official met him at 6 feet 4 and weighing more than 250 pounds, and he said Mr. Gaines was bigger than a house. The nickname stuck. Its symbolic richness came later.

After his graduation, he went to Winston-Salem Teachers College. He retired with 828 wins, placing him among the top five basketball coaches of all time. His Rams won one national title, in 1967. But these facts are not the reasons North Carolina is paying homage. Mr. Gaines was much more than a sports figure. He was also a mentor, friend, substitute parent and, during moments of frustration, drill sergeant for generations of young black men.

In his view, collegiate sports provided opportunities for high school graduates to improve their lives. Most of his players came from poor neighborhoods. Many had no father in their lives. Yet, with Coach Gaines' loyal and enthusiastic tutelage, over 80 percent of his players obtained their degrees from Winston-Salem. Growing up in Kentucky when racial segregation was still legal, Mr. Gaines witnessed countless moments of humiliation spawned by a country's hangover from slavery. Signs of progress, such as Jackie Robinson playing Major League Baseball or the passage of civil rights laws, were sporadic. To effect any positive influence required personal commitment. Throughout his early years, for example, the coach insisted that his players bear with grace the insult of having to sleep or eat in "colored only" quarters.

As his basketball teams improved, recruits began coming from different parts of the country and they began traveling to larger cities. Big House and his Rams quickly discovered that bigotry spanned all classes and social perspectives. Somehow, the blue bloods of snobbish New England and the hillbillies in the rural South shared a strange kinship. They could feel like nobility by looking down upon a common scapegoat.

The pretense of this decadent nobility is readily exposed when faced with the stature of someone such as Mr. Gaines. Reading his recent autobiography, *They Call Me Big House*, one is struck by how seldom he dwells on the rancor of bigots, whether they are small- town proprietors or big shots like University of Kentucky basketball coach Adolph Rupp. Coach Gaines instead evokes the image of the noble soul that philosopher Friedrich Nietzsche described. Such a soul is so magnanimous that he treats the taunts and slights as little more than annoying parasites who feed off the abundant vitality of their host.

When Nietzsche proclaimed, "O my brothers, I direct and consecrate you to a new nobility; you shall become begetters and cultivators and sowers of the future," he could have envisioned Big House Gaines. Mr. Gaines was too focused on cultivating the future to let past disappointments interfere.

Wherever Winston-Salem's athletic graduates are teaching, counseling, advising or helping today's youth, the imprint of "Big House" Gaines is seen. They know that nearly half of today's young black men are part of the criminal justice system. Without Mr. Gaines being part of their own lives, worse fates could have befallen them, too.

That's why North Carolina has paid homage to a basketball coach. And that's why an entire country should note this homage - as a way to celebrate a noble life.

Noted Baltimore Native Dies:
John Rawls—An Appreciation

John Rawls, a world-renowned philosopher and Baltimore native, has died. He grew up in Roland Park and eventually became a professor at Harvard University. He is most famous for his now-classic treatise, *A Theory of Justice*.

Since 1971 the book has been translated into dozens of languages and sold over 250,000 copies, a rare feat for a philosophy (or any academic) work. Conferences, journals and books from various disciplines have studied the implications and arguments of this book and Rawls' other writings. A recent journal ranked *A Theory of Justice* among the most important philosophy books in the twentieth century, sharing company with works by Wittigstein, Heidegger, Sartre, and Russell.

One reason for a particular philosophy's endurance is that people continually find new interpretations and insights. Even sincere readers of a text—be it a poem, story, legal brief, or sacred parable—can nevertheless draw contrary conclusions about its core tenets.

For *A Theory of Justice*, there were two core principles that anchored a just society. The first required equal and basic rights for everyone. The second, called the "difference principle," acknowledges that humans have uneven abilities and interests, and demands that basic goods (e.g., resources, opportunities, property) be distributed so that "any or all of these goods is to the advantage of the least favored." These principles acted less as utopian goals and more as standards or guides by which to judge moral and political progress.

Their meaning and relation to justice sparked considerable debate. In Rawls some critics saw a quasi- Marxist ,while others detected a subtle proponent of capitalism. Supporters found a framework of justice with universal potential; detractors countered that Rawls ignored marginal groups whose identities resisted assimilation.

As he wrote *A Theory of Justice*, Rawls was alert to his country being embroiled in Vietnam, waging a war on poverty, struggling heatedly over civil rights for blacks and women. He was also influenced by the wisdom of Aristotle on self-respect, of Kant on rationality and the social contract, of Mill on happiness and human nature, of Nietzsche on resentment and envy, and of many other significant thinkers.

What followed, instead, has been the treacle of self-esteem movements, a contract with America that cut taxes for multimillionaires without public principle, and mass consumption without self- assurance.

In Rawls' hometown, his obituary was preceded by news about CEOs of insurance companies receiving millions of bonus dollars while fewer citizens enjoy adequate health care, and public school officials were squabbling over six-figure salaries and administrative respect while thousands of children are undergoing an education unworthy of a modern democracy. Should these less fortunate recognize a just polity?

Rawls was obviously one of the more fortunate, and not only in terms of locale, family, and boarding school—he was clearly brilliant. J.B. Schneewind, philosopher and historian, tells of arriving at Princeton as a student and observing Rawls defend his doctoral dissertation. Such an ordeal can be a friendly ceremony, a rite of passage, or a blood bath exacted by barbarous professors. The young Rawls turned it into an erudite lesson by citing to the professors passages from Kant—in German!

Rawls' brother died at a young age. Nothing in Rawls' view could justify the arbitrariness of such misfortune. Indeed, so many of our advantages and disadvantages we are simply born with or fall into. Despite his many talents and the abstract tone of his writings, Rawls echoed some affinity for the venerable saying, "There but for the grace of God...."

Whether living in Roland Park, teaching at a college, working in downtown, exercising at the gym, taking in a game or concert, worrying about the stock markets, keeping an eye out on the kids—how many of us see the disparities and wonder about another's chance for a meaningful life? Which of us wind up accepting or seeking another form of polity?

A Happy, Grimm anniversary

*"The tales we tell each other and our children
not only reflect our own lived experiences and our
psychic realities, they also shape our lives."*
—Maria Tatar

As the year ends, we might appreciate a bicentennial that, unlike some wars, has been neglected in public circles. This modest event in 1812 was the publication of a book, titled *Children's and Household Tales.* We know it as "Grimms' Fairy Tales."

Assembled by two brothers, Jacob and Wilhelm Grimm, the book was a collection of short stories and tantalizing vignettes told and retold by generations of Germans. Though the brothers' original task was modest and scholarly—to study and preserve the richness of their own language—the tales have expectedly and continually fascinated generations of audiences. Even today they inspire commentaries, television programs and movies.

The reception of the Grimms' project has not been entirely positive. Feminists bemoan the denigration of the young lass passively waiting for her Prince Charming. Psychologists treat the tales as variants on children dealing with the stages of sexual development. Moralists view the tales as brief glimpses into social history where the characters embrace the social conventions, or transgress them at their own risk.

These and related perspectives offer a myopic approach to fairy tales. They overlook how the tales depict an extraordinary range of actions and emotions—from true love, courage and family devotion to cannibalism, harsh punishments and wanton cruelty to children. Their graphic portrayals of human triumph, tragedy and transformation make today's video games and reality television seem relatively tame and predictable.

Indeed, the Grimms' tales have universal appeal. With an uncanny ability to entertain while illuminating some tough realities, the tales magically interweave human experiences and imagination. For instance, stories of a pretty girl struggling against domestic and outside forces, as embodied in "Snow White," can be found throughout the world. The Grimms' version has the stepmother, jealous of her daughter's beauty, ordering the huntsman to kill the girl and bring back her lungs and liver—not just for proof of the deed but as part of the evening's dinner.

A recent gothic film starring Sigourney Weaver shows the Queen gloating and salivating in her cannibalistic endeavors. "Cinderella" (literally, the "girl among ashes") is a perennial rags-to-riches story found in many cultures. Audiences familiar only with the Disney movie, a feel-good tale where everyone eventually makes up, might be surprised to learn that in the Grimms' version, the envious sisters and the future bride of the prince do not cheerfully make amends and live in the castle. Instead, two pigeons who befriended Cinderella during her travails peck out the sisters' eyes, blinding them for life.

Before the advent of modern media, these tales were the material for everyday amusement and harsh lessons in life. According to eminent folklorists such as Maria Tatar and Jack Zipes, the stories rarely stayed exactly the same. Depending on the audience and milieu, the plot and characters would be constantly modified or embellished. For bedtime reading, parents might dramatize the consequences of a child who disobeys or wanders off the path (often into the unknown forest) and talks to strangers (usually portrayed by the big bad wolf). If regaled among drunken men in a local pub, though, the story would draw guffaws with bawdy twists and turns. Imagine the possible renditions of Little Red Riding Hood—from naive youngster and caring grandchild to lascivious temptress or femme fatale.

Simply put, Grimms' fairy tales have become a classic. The stock phrases that frame the tales—"Once upon a time" and "happily ever after"—are more than rhetorical devices. They emphasize that these stories could happen anywhere and anytime.

In this light, we can appreciate W. H. Auden's declaration that "these tales rank next to the Bible in importance." So long as the tales are told and retold, people will interpret and relive them in their own set of circumstances. Thus, the work of the Brothers Grimm carries its own sense of timelessness.

A Day to Honor
Bearers of Secrets

In today's employment section, there are few advertisements for secretaries. Employers instead seek administrative assistants, office technicians or multitasking receptionists. This embellishment of titles is unfortunate and misleading, for it erases the meaning of secretaries and their invaluable tasks.

"Secretary" shares etymological roots with "discreet," "discern" and "secrete." It derives from the word "secret," since secretaries have been expected to be discreet with all the information given them. Indeed, secretaries were centers of information long before the age of information. Notices of furtive interviews, rumors on new hires or firings, plans for surprise events, birth and death announcements and confidential memos—all pass by the secretary's desk.

Regardless of how salacious the news, the secretary has learned when to bite her tongue and seal her lips. The secretary is a master of silence, in sharp contrast to her supervisors. Lawyers, doctors or teachers, for example, are professionals paid to talk about what they know.

A secretary is paid not to talk about what she knows. As a result, an odd paradox ensues. With increased trust comes increased knowledge, so there is always more she must be silent about. This silence can be interpreted as an absence of advancement: She does the same work as before. Meanwhile, other professionals prattle on about the latest thing read, written or experienced, giving the impression that they are always advancing.

The effect of this paradox highlights a twofold injustice. First, it creates a common perception that secretaries have lesser intelligence than the ones for whom they work. Second, their pay is comparatively low, so they invariably look for better positions where their qualifications and education seem more profitable. Yet the secretaries I have worked with the most—Loretta Reynolds, Valerie Hollis, Debbie Blake, Carla Owens, Nicole Reese, the late Bernie Cochran—show an enviable amount of smarts. They know how to make newcomers feel welcome, quickly learn the latest computer programs that confound their supervisors, enlighten the room by finding the right word that brings a smile from others and deftly handle tasks dumped on them when one of those inevitable crunch times hits the office. Many times do they exercise their informed judgment and catch mistakes. That secretaries' wages rarely match the value of their contributions suggests another of capitalism's bad jokes.

Thus, cynics are tempted to dismiss Secretaries Day, which is today, as a symbolic but feeble gesture that glosses over this imbalance. These cynics believe that we should skip the cards or flowers and raise the pay instead. But this attitude overlooks that designating a day to honor someone—parents, veterans, laborers, presidents—has nothing to do with financial equity or compensation. Marking such a day is rather a cultural effort to express gratitude.

Philosopher Sissela Bok notes that secrets are an essential component of being human. Sharing a secret solidifies a friendship or initiates a sacred bond. While having the potential for harm, bearing secrets also involves some of our most positive virtues: trust, privacy, loyalty and practical wisdom.

In professional ethics, these virtues are often discussed about lawyers, doctors, scientists, teachers and clergy. In fact, secretaries best embody these virtues. They enable our workplaces to thrive and the rest of us to carry on with our work. As bearers of secrets, their tasks are often shrouded in silence. Secretaries Day gives us an opportunity to appreciate the positive value of that silence.

In his life, and ours:
Lennon at 70

*"I'm interested in expressing myself in a way that
will mean something to people in any country, in
any language, and at any time in history."*
—*From "Lennon Remembers"*

John Lennon would have been 70 tomorrow. The movie
"Imagine" will be aired as the tiresome, hagiographic view of
Lennon persists. Cynics will dismiss the birthday as another
pathetic occasion for baby-boomer nostalgia about the 1960s.
Some enthusiasts will remind us that Lennon was a rebel with a
cause - to be in a great rock band.

Although Lennon became one of the foremost artists of the
anti-war/social justice movements of the late 1960s and early
1970s, he was anything but a saint. His life was mostly a mix of
fascination, energy and trouble. An acerbic wit, quick to throw
a punch or perturb an adult, the young Lennon was never the
kid Liverpool's parents wanted to see with their own. Predictably,
teenagers were often drawn to Lennon's wild antics and compelling charm. Three of them - Paul McCartney, George Harrison
and Ringo Starr - disregarded their parents' fears and joined
Lennon to become The Beatles.

That he and the group still matter is why tomorrow's birthday is celebrated. Beatles' statistics reached Ruthian levels. Their
record for the most No. 1 singles and No. 1 albums is still unchal-
lenged. One week in 1964, they owned the top five singles on the
Billboard charts. Periodic surveys of the greatest 500 rock albums

invariably find The Beatles having five in the top 15. Incredibly, from 1965's "Rubber Soul" to 1969's "Abbey Road," they annually produced an album considered a classic by today's critics and fans. Perhaps only Beethoven's symphonies match such an accomplishment.

The Beatles remain the most revolutionary force in modern popular music. They first demonstrated the viability of an autonomous band whose members wrote, played and sang their own music. U2, the Dave Matthews Band, Green Day, REM - all are unthinkable without the Beatles. Even rap artists find inspiration in how the Beatles continually developed new sounds as they stopped touring and transformed into a studio group.

Lennon and his collaborators invented the rock album. They envisioned a collection of 12 to 14 songs that presented their best work rather than offering inferior material to back a hit song or two. Lennon and McCartney felt their fans should not pay twice for the same song, so they often left hit singles off their albums. The group saw each new album as an opportunity to experience and experiment with new sounds. A Beatles album was neither a sequel nor an afterthought - it was an event.

Some purists dismiss the Beatles as money-makers who sold out. They became the Fab Four or trippy eccentrics whom even parents could tolerate or enjoy. These purists might learn that when the Beatles went to Hamburg in 1960 to perform in its notorious Reeperbahn (a red light district), they began anticipating later forms of rock music. The striking film "Backbeat" depicts the Beatles in Hamburg as raucous and raw, mastering every form of rock 'n' roll and becoming forerunners to punk and grunge.

The Beatles were unabashed champions of American music. They admired Elvis Presley, Hank Williams, Buddy Holly and the Crickets (hence their name), and the girl groups of the early

1960s. With America mired in segregation, it was the Beatles - not the Rolling Stones or Bob Dylan - who convinced international audiences of the beautiful music being made by Ray Charles, The Shirelles and Smokey Robinson.

Current artists continue to be influenced by the Beatles. Gnarls Barkley says their music changed his life. His renowned Grey Album interweaves fragments of Beatles sounds and words with contemporary rhythms and beats. Win Butler, lead singer of Arcade Fire, whose CD "The Suburbs" just hit No. 1, remembers how listening to "A Day in The Life" evoked a different part of the universe.

In a 1970 interview, Lennon explained his love for Little Richard, Jerry Lee Lewis and Chuck Berry: "They're like primitive painters." Lennon and the Beatles, as disciples of such masters, became masters themselves through their own rebellious and creative musical paintings of the universe. The enduring richness of this mastery is why the band still matters and why John Lennon's birthday, 30 years after his untimely death, is still something to celebrate.

Villa Julie's Collaborators Retire After 30 Years

For Christine Noya

*Something was understood; the password among
accomplices was recognized. Something was said
that made you the accomplice of the one that is one
of his own kind: quetzal bird, savage, aboriginal,
guerilla, nomad, Mongol, Aztec, sphinx.*
—*Alphonso Lingis*

After 30 years at the helm, Villa Julie College's president Carolyn Manuszak is retiring. Reactions to the announcement have predictably praised her lengthy devotion to a college that has grown by leaps and bounds, from a junior college of a couple hundred girls to a four-year coed institution of a couple thousand students.

In my view, though, even more remarkable is her collaboration with Rose Dawson, the college's dean who is also retiring. For over 30 years--longer than most marriages and business partnerships--Carolyn Manuszak and Rose Dawson worked together to foster the life of Villa Julie College. Political obstacles, academic turf wars, neighborhood legal challenges, and financial resources sparked the many battles they waged together.

Undoubtedly they have had their share of victories and defeats. These experiences, however, never led them--as it often does for many shortlived collaborations--to boasting about personal credit for success and fingerpointing when things looked bleak. This is one of the many lessons true collaborators offer us. It is one we need to learn and appreciate because our lives benefit so much from their joint accomplishments. Political causes, religious movements, artistic endeavors, and scholarly pursuits take on a life not so much by the inspiration of a lone person but by the coordinated efforts of two or more talented and inventive individuals.

Collaborations thus help us exit the citadel of selfhood. It is misleading to conceive of them as partnerships that have a legally binding status. Manuszak and Dawson's collaboration has been an educational mission that continually animated their work. Personal gain, if any, was always a side effect rather than the purpose of their tasks. As any artist will confirm, once you start thinking about awards and million-dollar sellers, you stop doing art.

To account for the strength, beauty, and endurance of a collaboration is difficult.

Calling it "the right chemistry"---the popular metaphor these days--is a misuse of language. All the scientific expertise and genetic mapping in the world cannot explain or recreate two nuns in the mid-1960's taking over a religious institution and transforming it to become an established name in the secular world.

There is a magical and mysterious quality to a collaboration. It can be likened to an unpredictable mix of disparate components, such as the energy of a volcano joining the stable force of a mountain. Even these images fail to capture all that Carolyn Manuszak and Rose Dawson have accomplished. It is possible that we simply lack the language and values to understand and appreciate collaborations.

For ours is a culture that celebrates either the isolated individual or the financial empire. Joe DiMaggio is memorialized as an American legend even though he was incapable of sustaining a meaningful relationship with another human being. The Nike "swoosh" and McDonalds' golden arches are worldwide icons, symbolizing a worship of global mergers and acquisitions.

Yet it is the collaborators, not the isolated hero or the faceless conglomerate, who best exemplify the energies and aspirations of human experiences and dreams. It is they who contribute so much, in part by teaching us the value of working with others. Their accomplishments, if recognized and acknowledged, can free us of the cult of self-interest.

Every year announcements are issued about which individuals are selected for some hall of fame or which corporations get listed in the Fortune 500. Perhaps one day our culture will establish a pantheon of collaborators. Rogers & Hammerstein, Laurel and Hardy, Lennon-McCartney are among the recent candidates that come to mind.

To this list we might now add: Carolyn Manuszak & Rose Dawson.

2

Our Virtues, Our Vices

Introduction

For the longest time in ethics the theme of virtues and vices prevailed. Often considered a Christian theme, in fact the ancient Greeks and pagan writers discussed the nature of a virtue or vice before and independent of monotheistic religions such as Christianity. It seems most moral perspectives—be they religious or secular—contend that attention to virtues and vices is one of the means to improve individuals and societies.

Aristotle believed courage is the most fundamental virtue. Without it, efforts to embrace the other virtues were weak or shallow. Plato and Socrates frequently demeaned one of the most enduring vices—hubris (intellectual arrogance or vanity). Later the early Christian Fathers updated these ideas by formalizing a list of seven cardinal virtues and seven deadly sins.

Ask students to name one of the seven cardinal virtues (courage, justice, temperance, prudence from the pagans, and faith/ love, hope and charity from the Christians), they generally draw a blank. Ask them about the seven deadly sins, and within a minute or two they have identified them (pride, anger, envy, gluttony, lust, greed, sloth). They recall the movie "Seven", memories of their own experiences, or stories from television and movies.

The Essays

Sports have long been a part of my life—as participant, fan and little league coach. Though usually watching it, I've never been enthusiastic about the Super Bowl. The hype, opulent parties, record amounts of chicken wings sold, television audiences world-wide, superstar singers leading the half-time rituals, jet fighters soaring above the stadium as if war and football go together, all help celebrate the next four hours of what sports journalist Leonard Koppett calls a masterful illusion. As an opportunity for excessive indulgence, this annual winter Sunday ritual has taken on sacred proportions. Borrowing from the pagan gladiator battles and week-long festivals, this essay proposes that the Super Bowl has emerged as our modern spectacle.

Gambling is a perennial human pleasure and social danger. (Disclosure: I've been part of a modest poker circle for over 25 years.) The excitement of winning a fortune or losing one's worldly belongings has tempted generations from all parts of the world. While slot machines and commercial poker clubs have often been illegal and deemed a threat to family life, over the last decades public gambling has gradually been accepted. Indeed, to win the citizens approval for lotteries, casinos and their slot machines—which are little more than legalized theft—state governments such as Maryland promised the profits of casinos would make substantive contributions to the improvement of public schools. You be the judge on whether that promise has been fulfilled.

Paul McCartney wrote the most covered song of all-time, "Yesterday." He joined John Lennon to create the greatest musical band in The Beatles. His solo career is also quite impressive. Numerous number one singles and albums, sold-out concerts, and even a classical piece performed by the London Symphony Orchestra are among McCartney's post-Beatle highlights. In his recent book on collaborations, *The Powers of Two*, Joshua Shenk considers Lennon-McCartney to be one of the most formidable pairs ever. Yet Paul remains bothered that the Beatles' song credits are always "Lennon/McCartney." Is Paul's attempt to change these song credits a sign of vanity or proper pride? (A pop quiz: Find the references to Beatle songs in this essay.)

For generations Memorial Day and Labor Day marked the beginning and end of summer. Pools opened on Memorial Day weekend when school is almost over, while Labor Day signaled summer's last hurrah and the reopening of schools. That has changed as many school systems now begin a week before Labor Day (though Maryland's Governor Hogan recently moved school openings back after Labor Day). The nature of work has also changed. With stores now always open and computers quietly extending the hours we attend to our jobs, free time and work time have become blurred.

Sloth is the English term for the Latin seventh sin "acedia." It is the deadliest sin for it refers to spiritual apathy or melancholy, not just laziness. Its antithesis is purposeful freedom or deserved leisure—rewards of a responsible life. In op-ed essays citing one's sources is generally avoided (though the editor might ask an author if a certain claim can be verified). This essay was sparked and informed by Brigid Schulte's recent book, *Overwhelmed: Work, Love, and Play When No One Has the Time.*

The public fear of crime and actual crime rates have little correlation. If the news highlights two violent crimes committed by teenagers in the same week, invariably politicians start campaigning on "getting tough on juvenile criminals," even though official statistics show that over the last three years juvenile crime has actually decreased. The call for endless punishment presents a mix of virtues and vices. Anger can seem proper—we often speak of God's wrath, just retribution or righteous anger—yet its appearance as one of the deadly sins is attributed to anger's power to turn us into vengeful beasts who become blind to the suffering of others while exaggerating the wrong done to us. Keeping convicts institutionalized indefinitely borders on the vengeful beast route.

An argument can be made that no human being should be represented as a public statue. It risks idolatry and ignoring the human frailties or shortcomings of the person being commemorated. Such tension has been recently exemplified in the controversies over taking down statues in public parks, college campuses or government plazas. Since 1947 Baltimore had a statue of two Confederate officers, Robert E. Lee and Stonewall Jackson, sitting on their horses as they prepare for the next battle. Inscriptions below the statues praise Lee and Jackson's courage, honor, loyalty and Christian forthrightness. It does not mention that they were also fighting for the side that wished to continue slavery and advocated the innate inferiority of another race. This essay attempts a compromise. (Note: The statue was since removed by the City of Baltimore.)

There have always disputes about how, or even whether, school teachers can teach children to seek the good and avoid the bad. Former Mayor Martin O'Malley, facing budget cuts, contended that the arts should still be offered to the city's students. While he was lambasted by critics, the Mayor had considerable support from major thinkers who believe art is central to a child's education. Many philosophers, religious thinkers and scientific researchers agree that music, for example, fosters a sense of the sacred and an appreciation for harmony in the world as well as within oneself.

"Are We Willing to Risk our Flesh and Blood?" was reprinted in several newspapers, and maybe the first time I realized that some readers do take a second look at my writing. Though stirred by America's decision to invade Iraq (and soon Afghanistan), this essay addresses any decision that assumes some of our citizens will lose their lives so the rest of us do not risk ours. If humans are as rational as they claim to be, you would think they could find another way of resolving their disagreements without resorting to massive bloodshed. Borrowing from Elaine Scarry's *The Body in Pain* and Michel Foucault's lectures on defending society, this essay tries to highlight the tragic paradox in expecting fellow citizens to risk the ruin of their bodies for the security of our bodies.

Super Bowl: Roman Spectacle At Any Price

To excite, animate, enliven at any price—is that not the watch-word of an enervated, over-ripe, over-cultivated age? —Nietzsche

Super Bowl XXIX is here. We do not count our money as we count Super Bowls. Our computers, birth dates and anniversaries are not marked by Roman numerals. It seems odd how a country that rejects the metric system embraces strange and outdated numerical signs to name its biggest social event.

One theory holds that the NFL owners and television networks use Roman numerals to promote the classical status of the Super Bowl. Given the forgettable dullness of most of the games (quick: can you tell Super Bowl XIV from XIX?), one could argue that the Roman numerals have more to do with evoking the Roman Empire's enjoyment of spectacles that parallel our television spectacles. Or, what we might call telespectacles.

It is somewhat unfair that the Roman spectacles, a veritable orgy of sensations, are largely remembered for their bloody gladiator duels, which usually ended in a combatant's death. Our Super Bowl losers hardly fare so poorly, of course; they walk home with a day's pay most football fans only dream of. Still, we should not overestimate ourselves in depicting the barbarity of Roman spectators: They did not have the evening news to broadcast a local murder or foreign massacre.

The pleasures of ancient spectators ranged from the sounds of anguished cries and smells of splattered blood to the physical feeling of belonging to a drunken, unruly crowd. We telespectators have more modest pleasures: the aromas of microwaved popcorn, the drones of commentators, the comfort of our family rooms with the remote control lodged in our palms.

Another common feature is the universal appeal of spectacles. In Roman times, they were attended by people from all walks of life, including moralists and intellectuals. In his "Confessions," St. Augustine related the story of an educated friend who believed that his recent conversion could withstand the temptations of the spectacle. As Augustine feared, the friend reverted to the pleasures of gambling, drinking, cheering and booing the combatants, while eagerly awaiting the collapse and execution of the loser.

Our telespectacles demand comparable attention. Intellectuals who profess to be "above all that" still take in a Super Bowl, if only to have something to complain about with bored colleagues. People quite sincere in their ignorance about why the sport is called football will attend a Super Bowl party.

This attention demands time as well as space. The Roman spectacles could last several days, depending on extra festivities such as circuses or races. A football game is allotted 60 minutes, but we know better—even a two-minute warning draws out the suspense for a half-hour. In his study of leisure, Witold Rybczynski observes that Monday is probably the least productive work day because so many are recuperating from the hectic pace of the weekend's diversion. We telespectators are living proof. The mind is numbed, the body stiff from unnatural postures, the digestive system cleansing itself from chips, dip and light beer, and the eyes still blurred from dazzling commercials and too many close-ups of superhuman athletes sweating, spitting and snarling.

The value of advertisers, by the way, is crucial, far transcending the 30-second blips that cost a half-million dollars or so. Like the statues of the pagan gods prominently surrounding the coliseum that was host to gladiator duels and human tortures, advertisers cast an eye on the whole scene, as if they are appreciating and judging the human drama unfolding before them. The commercials that fill Super Bowl slots say very little about the products themselves. Instead, they are full of creative, humorous and stunning visual snippets, often compensating for the lack of suspense on the field.

Sportswriters and fans are predicting and betting who will win, by how much, and whether the XLIX'ers will turn the game into another soporific slaughter. About these things I have no idea. But I would wager that Super Bowl XXIX will rank among the top X televised shows of all time, right up there with other Super Bowls. And Monday morning DJs will rehash the event to stir up the semi-slumbering drivers jammed in rush-hour traffic.

Like pagans, we may be so enervated that we cannot ignore our telespectacles. To have them, our society will spend billions of dollars, squander immense amounts of gasoline and electricity, use up tons of plastic wrapping and metal containers, expend hours and days of physical and mental energy. Again, from a rational economic view, it does not add up. Perhaps Nietzsche knew what economists do not: We need to be excited by something at any price.

Let's Profit from Slots and Other Vices

"Thus every part was full of vice, Yet the whole mass a paradise." —Bernard Mandeville (1705)

Opponents of the referendum to legalize slots in Maryland should fold their collective hands. Supporters of the referendum, from the governor and education officials to casino and horse track owners, are too formidable.

Instead of further resistance, opponents of slots might better engage in oneupsmanship. Not only join the bandwagon, but also ask: Why stop here? The pleasure in greed, a driving force to gambling, has long been one of the deadliest vices in social and religious traditions. If it can be twisted into a public virtue because it ostensibly will help education, lower tax rates and promote local historical traditions, then perhaps we should consider how other vices can profit Marylanders.

We could start with the lust-ridden Block. While moralists condemn its celebration of carnal pleasures or promotion of sexist indulgences, Baltimore's historians invariably highlight the Block's legendary reputation and its most famous figure, Blaze Starr. To pre-empt neighboring states who might tempt our lust-driven citizens, Maryland could establish more Blocks. For convenience, they could be adjacent to all the fake Avenues that now dot the shopping mall landscape.

Customers ogling a dancer's writhing body will be gratefully reminded that a portion of their $7 for a can of beer will be earmarked for the public good. The next step might be legalizing prostitution, where clients could be charged additional user fees to subsidize textbooks on sex education.

Anger is another vice with profit potential. The state penitentiary in downtown Baltimore has historical significance. Yet, like all prisons, it can be a drain for taxpayers who mostly resent any humanitarian gesture for convicts. A shrewd government could exploit the anger-management crises afflicting its citizens by resurrecting the spectacle of public punishment.

M & T Bank Stadium, with more than 70,000 seats, is used only about 10 times per year for Ravens games. Whereas football is seasonal, anger is year-round. Bimonthly public punishments should be easy moneymakers for the state. To soothe spectators' conscience, large video screens in the stadium could show how portions of the proceeds are devoted to various juvenile delinquency programs. Once legalized, the only difficulty lies in sorting out prices for beheadings, tortures or impalements.

Once these precedents have been set, Maryland's government could turn its attention to other vices. Perhaps it could find profit by connecting gluttony to taverns and restaurants, or sloth to television and movie theaters. Indeed, once some enterprising and imaginative legislators find a way to milk our thirstiest and most pernicious vices — pride and envy — Maryland could be a tax-free state.

So for the next election, foes of the slots ought to stop all this pettifoggery about the referendum's language. The lottery did not save public schools, and neither will casinos. Only by profiting from all the vices can Maryland finally become a citizen's paradise.

Let It Be, Paul

He has more No. 1 singles and albums than any other musician. His "Yesterday" is the most recorded song in history. He has been knighted and received a coat of arms. Major orchestras have performed his classical compositions. And in Rolling Stone magazine's last poll on the 100 greatest rock 'n' roll albums, his group, the Beatles, placed four in the top six, with Revolver voted No. 1. Yet Paul McCartney is worried about his legacy.

Though starting work on a new album, he has also been trying to revise some old song credits to read McCartney- Lennon rather than Lennon-McCartney. This could more accurately reflect whether he or his brilliant partner, John Lennon, was chief writer of a particular song. (Mr. Lennon, who was shot to death Dec. 8, 1980, would have been 63 today.)

Current generations of Beatles fans are not the concern - they already know whether "Help," "Hey Jude" or "She Loves You" is a joint effort or primarily penned by one or the other.

The concern is over Mr. McCartney's legacy among future generations. There appears a gnawing sense that his contributions will be forgotten when tomorrow's listeners hear Beatles music, casually noting that Mr. Lennon and some partner wrote them.

This involves a peculiar human paradox. Don't most of us wonder what we have accomplished and how we'll be remembered? Teachers hope, but rarely ascertain, that they really educated students and not just helped them satisfy their requirements. Parents do their utmost to give a child memorable times and opportunities but hear no reply if curious about a final assessment.

Humility or modesty aside, gaining credit intrigues us. When carving initials on a tree trunk, etching names in fresh concrete, deciding an official moniker for a written or artistic work, tagging a graffiti signature or designing the epitaph for one's gravestone, humans announce something about themselves to others. This something could be what I experienced, you thought, he imagined or she created. We call attention to something in silence for a tomorrow when others come upon our name and we can no longer speak. Of this tomorrow one never knows.

Though a billionaire, Paul McCartney realizes not only that money can't buy love, but also that it can't guarantee a legacy. Critics often undermine the commercial and creative success of the Beatles. Their lyrics lack the edge and social conscience of Bob Dylan. Or they were seduced by artistic indulgence, abandoning the rocking purity and radical outrage that characterized Elvis or the Rolling Stones. Phony Beatlemania, charged the Clash.

These and similar comparisons are facile. They overlook how the Beatles were the most controversial and revolutionary of all. Long before punk or rap, Beatles' records were vilified in religious conflagrations, their concerts spawned pandemonium and spectacle, their songs, which expanded endlessly the possibilities of subsequent musicians, were banned by radio stations. The infamous "Butcher Block" cover protested EMI/Capitol's carving up of their albums.

More importantly, these comparisons ignore how enduring and fecund Lennon-McCartney music has been. Stevie Wonder, Elton John and Banarama topped the charts with their songs. Reggae artists and New Wave performers have also covered them. The movie I Am Sam offers a soundtrack of Beatles tunes, sung by current luminaries that include Sheryl Crow, Eddie Vedder of Pearl Jam, and Sarah McLachlan.

In this light, tinkering with the credit lines could diminish rather than enhance Mr. McCartney's legacy. Experts or (worse) legalists might then propose Lennon-McCartney by Mr. Lennon's masterpieces such as "Strawberry Fields," "Forever," "I Am the Walrus" or "Girl." Worse, it threatens to tarnish their unique legacy - a collaboration that spans the ages.

After Edmund Hillary and Tenzing Norgay scaled Mount Everest, Mr. Hillary refused to say who first touched the peak. Neither could have reached the summit without the other. He understood that each of us, regardless of the significance of our own accomplishments, always gets by with a little help from our friends.

Paul McCartney - with John Lennon - created a musical Everest: the Beatles. When mortality takes away his voice, it will be the legacy of Lennon-McCartney that speaks to future generations. Manipulating that credit betrays Mr. McCartney's remarkable gifts, illustrating vanity rather than pride. Words of wisdom, Paul: Let it be.

Stop laboring on Labor Day

Ask some neighbors or colleagues about their Labor Day weekend tomorrow, and prepare to hear how busy it was. Several malls featured back to school sales, kids had a baseball tournament, lots of e-mails to catch up with at work, and the house needed some cleaning. We're too busy, goes the lament, to enjoy free time.

Yet social scientists claim that the average work week for full-time employees since 1970 has fluctuated between 39 and 41 hours. This claim does include a range of variations. For every doctor or police officer who puts in an extra shift, there is a nurse or computer technician who puts in three 12-hour days or four 9-hour days. The point is that more and more people claim they have less free time while statistics show that time at the workplace is about the same as for our parents and grandparents.

Several factors might account for this discrepancy. One, sometimes we just like to complain or embellish. We want others to know that what we do is so important or meaningful. Weekends have a purpose, vacations are educational, school breaks are structured, and kids are supported at extracurricular events—with parents in dutiful attendance to shout "good job."

Fueling these accounts is the sense that "24/7" is the new normal. Ostensibly labor-saving technologies appear to have misled or beguiled us.

Take technology for example. Instead of providing more leisure, computers and the Web and social media are among so many e-venues that promise to save work while actually creating more of it. With the Internet, shopping, updating LinkedIn profiles, checking investment opportunities or researching better ways to raise your kids are always within reach—as are time-eating lists of worst animal breeds and cute baby videos. They often occupy the busy moments of days like today, which is meant to be free.

We are never "off" anymore, with email and Twitter and Facebook readily accessible right on our phones. We check messages on vacation and during cocktail hours, in case a supervisor has raised a last-minute concern; and we read headlines while watching our kids play.

The separation of work and play, both in terms of time and space, has become blurred. Labor Day, originally meant to honor workers with a new leisure day, is no longer a break from being busy. It is a continuation.

The car too is a culprit in this. People drive more than ever. The typical 15-minute commute in 1970 has turned into an hour commute. Traffic congestion is no longer limited to rush hour, as weekend roads are jammed with shoppers, travelers, truckers and parents hauling their kids to sundry events. Hours in the car neither counts as work time nor as leisure time. Even if we tend to exaggerate our sense of being busy, there is considerable evidence that leisure time in American culture has eroded.

Perhaps a small step toward countering this: a day (or weekend) of sloth. Sloth has a notorious reputation. Early moralists considered it the deadliest of the classic seven deadly sins. Its Latin term, "acedia," meant lack of uplifting purpose or spiritual direction. Benjamin Franklin conferred on time financial worth, so to waste time was to waste money. And children for centuries have been told that idle hands are the devil's tool kit, of which today's casinos are a perfect illustration.

Sloth, however, has its virtues. It speaks of a time that belongs to us. Many artists, scientists and scholars claim that some of their best insights arrived when idle, day dreaming or taking a walk. We might restore the sense of sloth that is, according to historian

Aviad Kleinberg, optimistic. It respectfully encourages fellow citizens to enjoy a sense of free time without designed purposes and lasting rewards.

And this enjoyment is unplugged to Internet, auto traffic and work.

Replacing Labor Day with Sloth Day could be a modest step toward reviving the valuable time of leisure when we can do anything we want—or do nothing at all.

An Endless Punishment?

If Maryland officials implement recently discussed plans, many individuals guilty of sex crimes will complete their sentences and then will be required to enter a psychiatric institution.

This idea invites interminable punishment by reviving efforts to combine the legalization and the medicalization of criminal issues. It offers to protect us from a horrible deed and seek revenge for it. But it could easily compound a horror with further injustice and greater confusion and suffering. Consider: First, there is the assumption of a special connection between sex and crime. While sex and crime are reliable sellers for movies and pop songs, specialists in criminal justice often note the arbitrariness in this connection. Other crimes generate considerable damage without any basis in sex.

Indeed, many laws are broken by those who are greedy, jealous, intolerant or just plain ornery. Yet no official proposes that offenders such as the money-hungry executive, suspicious spouse or enraged bigot undergo psychiatric institutionalization after serving their allotted time in prison.

Second, whatever the possible link between sex and crime, it is doubtful coercive medical or psychiatric approaches will help. The notoriety of a Jack the Ripper or 1970s serial killer Ted Bundy is misleading insofar as experts have trouble explaining these individuals. Sure, most tend to be males. Often, and unpredictably, the offender is from one's own family, school, workplace or neighborhood.

In a remarkable study, medical historian Simon Cole shows that sex offenders were called psychopaths in the 1950s. These could include exhibitionists, masturbaters and peeping Toms—commonplace among today's Internet users. That today's offenders are called predators is not accidental. By conjuring images of a wild beast, experts imply that the tools of criminal justice are insufficient to calm a fearful citizenry. According to Mr. Cole, however, specialists remain divided on two fundamental issues: an accurate diagnosis and a reliable cure for an offender.

A third problem concerns precedent. Some researchers claim to have found a DRD2 gene that is associated with pathological gamblers. When these gamblers get caught stealing to feed their habits, should prison then become only a holding place until they get proper medical care?

Numerous researchers find a link between testosterone and aggression. This could account not only for the urban violence local television features to entice its audiences, but also the destruction from commuter traffic in neighboring counties. Perhaps the road rage of all those suburbanites hustling around in their SUVs is better controlled not by police but by medical technicians periodically stopping commuters to check if their testosterone levels are dangerously out of whack.

Finally, to further institutionalize a convict who has served his time in prison creates the impression that punishment is no longer guided by a sense of deterrence, retribution or some other distinct end. That is, the state can now punish endlessly.

The possibility of endless suffering is quite different from other possible painful experiences. Most of us dwell on the suffering that seems never to quit: Lingering grief or broken heart, loss of freedom or squelched hopes, missed opportunities or the miseries of others. Endless pain seems excessive, inexplicable and unjustifiable. Some liken it to torture.

So to inflict that kind of pain should worry any people of a democracy. That our country has numerous executions and 2 million prisoners should be alarming enough. We are planting seeds for a culture that consigns any miscreant to endless punishment.

Politically Incorrect Statues
Provide a Teachable Moment

In Spain reformists are calling for the removal of any public recognition of the Surrealist master, Salvador Dali, because he was an ardent supporter of the Franco fascist regime. In the Middle East, the Taliban and ISIS destroyed ancient Buddhist statutes and sacred monuments they claim are false idols and sources of evil. And here in the U.S., people are demanding the removal of Confederate symbols because of their links to our slave past.

With that in mind, a Baltimore task force has begun holding meetings to decide the fate of several renowned monuments in the city. Like their predecessors in other parts of the world, this group assumes the authority to decide which parts of our history should be displayed or concealed from fellow citizens.

Such a task poses a peculiar threat to public life and civic discourse if it neglects the following: First, the statues are artistic achievements, meant to be experienced as part of the public commons rather than confined to museum rooms or warehouses of taboo items. Second, as with most sacred figures, the statues inspire reflection; they greet passersby with compelling scenes that deserve two or three looks. And third, perhaps most important, these works of art invite visitors to their own teachable moments, which educators relish as the unexpected experience that provokes curiosity and renewed insight.

For example, consider one of the best known statues in Baltimore—the Lee and Jackson monument in Wyman Park, across from the Baltimore Museum of Art. It is a stunning sculpture. A couple of visitors from Annapolis saw it and remarked that it is the kind of statue one might find in Paris or Vienna. It is the 1946 work of Laura Fraser (alert, the "u" is etched as a "v"), among first female sculptors to achieve national fame.

Imagine students, joggers, travelers or area residents on an evening stroll happening upon Fraser's creation. Surrounded by trees, amid local traffic, with distant sounds of the dog park or vendors yelling "ice cold" to commuters wanting a bottle of chilled water, they stand before this monument. They look up at the larger-than-life figures of Stonewall Jackson and Robert E. Lee on their horses and stand in awe.

Yet there is more to this artistic work than just the figures. The inscriptions surrounding this statue also draw our attention. They indicate that the scene is Jackson and Lee parting ways as they prepare for the battle of Chancellorsville. Then there are the words describing them: "great generals," "Christian soldiers," and "waged war like gentlemen." Also evident is Jackson's admission that his confidence in Lee is such that he would "follow him blindfolded."

Here the teachable moment arises. With a quick check on a smartphone most people with a sense of curiosity can begin weighing some questions. If Lee and Jackson are great generals, then why did their side lose? Christianity preaches forgiveness and loving thy neighbor, so how could these soldiers trying to kill their northern neighbors be true followers of Jesus? And what does it mean for a gentleman to wage war? Do non-gentlemanly military tactics look any different? Visitors to this remarkable sculpture might then recall visits to nearby battlefields, such as Antietam or Gettysburg, where they witnessed accounts and re-enactments of the massive slaughters each side enforced and suffered.

Thousands of American lives lost in less than a week. The stench of burning flesh and agonizing sounds of lingering death for days seem to mock or undermine any association of a gentleman with war.

These sorts of images and words present viewers of the Lee/Jackson statue an opportunity to learn and reflect. While no mention of slavery, the South or states' rights is mentioned at this site, viewers can readily check their electronic gadgetry and discover how these issues were part of the historical landscape. They can also gaze at this statue to consider and ponder the endless human tragedies and paradoxes provoked by warfare. They might appreciate or dispute the extent of the wisdom, courage or loyalty embodied by those who fought and the willingness to kill or die for their side.

These teachable moments can arise with many of Baltimore's monuments. Those wearing the mantle of faux sensitivity and insincere tolerance in order to demand that these statues be removed from the public commons betray considerable hubris. They assume most of us are too fragile or simple-minded to appreciate and understand these works of art on our own terms.

Are we willing to commit our flesh and blood?

There is an art to getting the answers you want by phrasing questions in the right way.

For example, ask about 2,000 citizens (sufficient for a scientific sampling) if the United States should invade Osama bin Laden-friendly Iraq and its demonic tyrant, Saddam Hussein, and even pacifists would be hard-pressed to answer no.

That the news media and the Bush administration have cited polls showing Americans support a military attack on Iraq is, in this light, hardly compelling. To ask about overtaking a country whose culture, history and language few of us understand is tantamount to a talk show soliciting callers' opinions about, say, firing the manager of the local team, replacing incumbents in City Hall or changing school mascots.

If the media and President Bush were genuinely interested in whether Americans support a military occupation of another country, they should ask citizens a different question, to wit:

If you support a military invasion of Iraq and replacement of Saddam Hussein, are you willing to: Enlist in one of the armed services? Encourage your son or daughter to join the military? Renew a draft of all 18-year-olds? How does this kind of question change things? According to Elaine Scarry, in her seminal work *The Body in Pain*, humans are limited in their capacity to verbally persuade one another.

Eventually, disagreement over convictions eludes rational deliberation. Ultimate differences can be settled only with the flesh, pain and blood of one another's bodies. Applied to the current crisis, if we are convinced that American ideals of freedom or justice are at stake, then we should be willing to offer our own bodies, or at least those of relatives or neighbors.

Evidence of this willingness is remarkably absent. Military officials report no unusual increase of recruits since Sept. 11. Neither Mr. Bush nor Congress, regardless of their saber rattling, dare lose votes by proposing a resurrection of a mandatory draft. And pundits, from conservatives such as Mona Charen to leftists such as Christopher Hitchens, have dodged this question entirely while parading under the pro-invasion banner.

One explanation for this obduracy is that an all-volunteer army has insulated us from the horrors of war. Video games and Hollywood - - the usual scapegoats—are blameless for this insular effect. More likely, knowing that fellow citizens choose a career in the armed forces deludes the rest of us into the notion that we need not join them when the going gets tough.

This delusion rests on an historical anomaly. A scholar on civil- military relations, sociologist James Burk, points out that an all- volunteer army cannot alone sustain a lasting war. Sooner or later it requires the physical support, not just the lip service, of the citizenry. Whether stagnant on the front lines, holed up in make-shift shelters, or scouting the area for snipers or guerillas, soldiers tend to reach a threshold.

To displace Mr. Hussein, American soldiers can expect a lengthy presence, making them vulnerable to counterattacks from loyalists and patriots. Though Mr. Hussein has been painted as a villain in the likes of Hitler or Stalin, we should not forget how they nevertheless garnered the devotion of some of the population. That means millions of potential threats lurking about in a country the size of Iraq.

Hence, the question posed to Americans should be more direct. And if you or I hem or haw about the unlikelihood of our physical contribution, then we are doing more than underestimating the myriad repercussions possible in the Middle East. We are also denying our own civic responsibility.

Being unwilling to offer our flesh and blood is tantamount to confessing that overtaking Iraq has nothing to do with democracy or freedom. If content that a volunteer army should suffer all the wounds and casualties for this enterprise, then we are donning the mantle of an international ogre who consigns its soldiers to mercenary status. Such a scenario involves more than the slogan that talk is cheap or that the Bush administration is committed to satisfying our appetite for cheap energy. Rather, it indicates that Americans desire a still stranger bargain—war on the cheap.

3
Promises and Pitfalls of Science

Introduction

Apparently I was the last professor on my campus to use a computer. There was an informal poll over which faculty used the least amount of technology in their pedagogy, and I had the dubious honor of winning. Such recognition implies one is a throwback and resists advances in science and technology.

To question scientific optimism invariably invokes the charge of being a Luddite. This is somewhat unfair, as the Luddites were not against advances in machinery and technology, but against the possibility that these advances would take away their livelihood. For a number of years my college offered a series of courses on "Humanities and Technology." One of those was "Philosophy and Technology." While initially reluctant to teach this course (as I was unfamiliar with many emerging technologies), I'm now thankful for this opportunity because it pushed me to engage in a recurring philosophical question—what's going on now?

Science and technology, as much as religion and politics, have presented the most drastic changes in our lives. In the 1960s the pioneer of media analysis Marshall McLuhan anticipated how advocates would promise that the newest means of communication will advance the likelihood of a global village, one in which peoples from various cultures and distant lands could learn about and accept one another. McLuhan was also a skeptic and would likely be unsurprised that despite today's social media, the human species might be more fragmented than ever. Pitfalls invariably continue to arise.

The Essays

When cell phones first became available to the general public about twenty five years ago, people said having one was important in case of a rare emergency. That view now seems quaintly ancient, as cell (or smart) phones are now ubiquitous. (Full disclosure and shameful confession—I do not have a cell phone.) Whether they enhance or undermine human civility and community remains unsettled. The first essay in this chapter was initiated by seeing a father so focused on a cell phone that he was oblivious to the sobs of his four year old daughter. This essay drew many favorable responses, especially from those involved in education or child care whose experiences with cell-phone culture were more extensive than mine.

Drones are also becoming a part of our everyday lives. Realtors, military, police, traffic officials boast about the advantages of drones. Yet they have also become quite useful for criminals and those who want to spy on their fellow citizens. Since this essay was published, the use of drones has steadily increased, be it delivering pizzas or carrying terrorist arsenal. And forthcoming might be a drone speed race, whose fans want it to be considered as a competitive sport. Imagine five years from now, and leading the sports news are two obese nerds, incapable of walking a 40 yard dash or doing five jumping jacks, but they do have the fastest thumbs to guide their drones to the finish line.

Drones, cell phones and other technological innovations are part of the growing concerns that individual or group privacy is more endangered than ever. The Fourth Amendment in the Bill of Rights is arguably one of the most distinct political statements in modern history. When applauding its importance, Benjamin

Franklin admitted that it will be continually challenged or threatened. This amendment does not use the actual word "privacy." It does emphasize how one has the right to not have his personal property (home, farm, apartment, physical body) subject to search or seizure by a government or central authority. "Farewell to Privacy?" was the editor's headline for this essay. Mine's was pedantic, "Privacy versus Security—the Enduring Struggle". I much prefer the editor's more ominous rendition.

Many of these disputes are obviously fueled by the stunning emergence of the computer and artificial intelligence. The speed, accuracy, ability to calculate in seconds what would require hours for a human mind all have clearly demonstrated the undeniable powers of the computer (or robot). The editor's title, "Does Watson Put Humanity's Future in Jeopardy" reflected his delightful play on words. Watson refers to the computer that defeated long-time Jeopardy (the popular game show) champion Ken Jennings. Watson was programmed by MIT computer wizards, so it might be inaccurate to say that it is simply computer versus reigning Jeopardy champion.

How these notions affect our basic understanding of humanity is the underlying theme. Are humans little more than embodied brains that function like computers? If so, then maybe we should welcome an artificial intelligence machine that functions more quickly, efficiently and reliably than the human brain machine, be it deciding on who to love or when to wage war. On the other hand, are you and I willing to accept the claim that we are basically machines?

One response is that a unique characteristic of human beings has nothing to do with intelligence or reasoning. Instead, our species is distinct insofar as we produce more garbage than any other species on the planet. Worse, the waste of animals in nature is recycled and part of life while the waste of humans is not. Human garbage has contaminated lakes, rivers and oceans. It has clogged bays and harbors, endangering the water and air supplies of fellow humans, mammals and fishes throughout the planet. Plastic epitomizes this threat, for it can take hundreds of years to disintegrate while other creatures inhale or eat the molecules that survive from discarded plastic bags and bottles. Admittedly, I'm just as culpable when considering the amount of garbage I place in the back alley for the trash collectors.

"Weapons of Greatness" was developed in light of our country's invasion of Iraq. The rationale was based on the allegation that Iraq harbored "weapons of mass destruction." It turned out, despite the US government's insistence that Iraq was ready to unleash chemical or nuclear weapons, nothing was found. At the time I had been reading several things about how all the world's great powers possessed overwhelming weapons to conquer its hapless victims. The unstoppable horsemen of Genghis Khan, ruthless soldiery of Sparta, intimidating onslaught of the British navy, atomic bombs used by the USA and possessed by the world's dominant countries, all reflect that powerful and ruthless weapons of mass destruction are integral to those countries we also consider great.

It was happenstance that I was two blocks away from what was potentially major disaster. A train tunnel in central Baltimore had an accident where several cars were so damaged that they released all sorts of smoke, fumes, and chemicals. City officials were not prepared for the possible emission of poisonous gases floating into neighborhoods and roads. They ordered local apartment buildings to be evacuated, streets completely shut down and residents head for safe shelter. It was a city in chaos. Luckily the leakage from the damaged train cars was not lethal. But the threat was genuine. It showed that Baltimore needed to evaluate the economic benefits of having a variety of trains moving through its streets versus the possibility of a major accident threatening its own citizens. Politicians often talk about the infrastructure of cities, bridges, tunnels and highways, but implementing actual policies and plans is a more difficult matter.

The severity of AIDS was not obvious in its earliest stages. At first it was suspected to be a gay cancer that was spread through promiscuous night clubs where anonymous sex was condoned or encouraged. When famous people such as tennis star Arthur Ashe contacted AIDS through blood transfusions, the public quickly realized that the disease was spread through the exchange of vital body fluids. That is when health officials decided to extend their attention to heroin addicts and assure their shared needles were sterile.

By chance I was traveling through Switzerland while Zurich was initiating the first needle exchange programs in its most prominent public park. The clerk at the train station frowned when I asked, as if annoyed over this voyeuristic interest in Needlepark. It was a short walk from the train station to discover young people barely able to stay on their feet with needles dangling from their necks, since the veins of their arms were all used up. Older men were scouting out young female addicts. Friends were trying to keep their heroin-addicted buddies from collapsing. Some addicts had crashed and looked like the grim reaper had taken them. Back home I learned that Baltimore City was deliberating whether to establish a Needlepark near downtown. To me, it conjured images of a human zoo rather than a site for humane treatment.

Seeking a new tourist attraction, Baltimore's leaders worked out a surprising sports spectacle—a Grand Prix race through the city's downtown district. Considerable energy and expense was devoted to this race. To comply with racing regulations, many of downtown's streets had to be restructured so that drivers were safe to make sharp turns when zipping along at 80 or 90 miles per hour. This caused daily traffic jams in downtown.

Many of my comments were informed by the sports pages and a good friend, John Duggins. He is a big fan of car racing, even going to Florida once a year to see some major race. John's a smart guy, so I always wondered about his attraction to this sport. He chuckled at my snobbish attitude and sometimes described how going to these races was a very exciting experience. This essay drew a number of irritated responses. Some wondered what I had against fun or the city trying to promote itself. Most memorable was a reader who asked if he could offer two opera tickets to me and my husband. These sarcastic rejoinders did not have the last laugh. The event died after two races.

Try putting down your cellphone and picking up your kid

At the local pool there is a 3-year-old crying. She sobs for 30 seconds, trying to gather herself and articulate a word or two about what is bothering her. Traditionally in such a situation, a stranger or life guard would approach the toddler and immediately ask, "Where is your mommy or daddy?"

Not any longer. The father is right there, slouched in his lounge chair, sitting 3 feet from his daughter, who stands on the sidewalk in tears. He does not look or talk to her. His eyes are glued to a cellphone.

One can only guess what might be more important than his upset toddler. Perhaps he is checking the latest reports on the stock market, updated baseball scores, a potential rendezvous on hook-up sites. Maybe he is doing a search on Google with the subject line "What to do when your 3-year-old daughter is crying and you don't feel like dealing with it."

This is not an isolated anecdote. Walking through a public park, I see a 2-year-old boy delighting in his newfound mobile talents. He's not just walking, but now running, climbing and jumping. Excitedly he asks his parents to look at what he can do. But he needs to ask again, as they are focused on their cellphones.

Stopping by a family restaurant, there's a table of five: grandmother, parents and two children. The young ones looked bored and restless, until one of the adults hands them their cellphone to share something amusing.

Today's students who work as babysitters or nannies attest to the frequency of a parent returning home and paying more attention to their phone, which has presumably been with them all day, than their kids, who haven't.

What this means for a toddler is unclear. A child is a sponge for new experiences. How she or he absorbs the moment when seeking the attention of a parent only to be rebuffed by a tiny electronic gadget is an open question. Perhaps there will be funded research on the possible ramifications of this growing phenomenon. "The Post-Traumatic Symptoms of a Cell-Phone Abandoned Child" or "Why do Ma and Pa Love It more than Me?"

Harry Chapin's classic hit, "Cat's In the Cradle" offers some instruction. It was an unusual song to hit number one on the Billboard singles charts in the 1970s. Chapin sings about a son who adores his father. Kid wants to be just like him. The father, though, is too focused on work and personal tasks to play ball or take walks with his son. As the son becomes an adult, the father's hectic life slows down a bit, and he seeks some moments together with his son. Sorry, Dad, the song goes, "my new job's a hassle, and the kid's got the flu, but sure nice talking to you." In other words, the son has become like his dad - can't make time and space for him. And that was before cellphones.

Soon we might hear an updated version of Chapin's touching lament. Once children reach the age when they can have their own cellphones, the parents will ask for an afternoon together with the children face-to-face, hoping to see hope and humor in their eyes, to hear their vibrant voices. "Not today," the children will text back. "Text me next month and see if there is a break in my busy calendar."

"The child is innocence and forgetfulness, a new beginning, a sport, a self-propelling wheel, a first motion, a sacred Yes," - Friedrich Nietzsche in "Thus Spoke Zarathustra"

Nietzsche's aphorism conveys a spiritual or recurring truth about childhood. It is not just a stage between infancy and adulthood. The child who laughs or cries is expressing the innocence of youth, the energy of a self-propelling wheel and a momentary sacred "yes" to the surprises and disappointments of being alive.

When a toddler brings his or her joy or sorrow to you, the parent, it is an effort to share this innocence and energy. To ignore this and stare at a cellphone is a violation against your child's sacred yes.

The Drones are Coming

*Prepared for the next invasion? It will not be led
by foreign terrorists or illegal immigrants. This
invasion will come in the form of drones
—An American specialty Promo.*

A judge has ruled that the Federal Aviation Agency cannot ban from public airspace flying robots or pilotless air vehicles owned by commercial enterprises. This decision means drones will no longer be used primarily for war or border patrols. They will soon become part of everyday life.

Advocates anticipate a veritable panacea. Drones will be the next dominant industry, generating billions of dollars and thousands of jobs. Their humanitarian efforts will be welcome for farmers checking on their crops and rescue teams scouting for lost children or hikers stranded on a mountain. Companies are preparing to deliver packages via drones instead of clogging the streets with trucks and vans.

This enthusiastic embrace of the latest flying gadget seems shortsighted. It neglects to recognize how any new technology—regardless of its inventor's intentions—can be used in a variety of unexpected ways. For example, when Henry Ford offered an affordable and reliable car for the average American, he did not anticipate a grateful letter from the infamous thief Clyde Barrow because his Model-T was faster than the police cars. Designers of the cellphone could hardly have predicted its use in detonating bombs in public areas.

Drone advocates neglect additional features looming on the horizon. First, drones will be arriving in all sizes and shapes. Newspapers and television tend to illustrate drones resembling those toy airplanes that flew in endless circles. Drones are acrobatic machines, capable of being maneuvered amid trees in forests and buildings dotting an urban skyline. Some are called micro-aviaries, as they can emulate the motions of hummingbirds. Scientists are now completing work on nano-drones, which will masquerade as bees or houseflies. Not to worry. The naked eye will not recognize them, unless they travel in swarms.

Second, drone advocates neglect to address how humans will use their flying robots to resolve disagreements and conflicts. Hunters have begun deploying drones to find their targets. This is illegal, according to members of PETA, who want their drones to protect the animals or identify the miscreants. The idea of neighbors or criminals obtaining their own drones presents obvious problems. One engineer from a Utah avionics laboratory acknowledges that considerable research is already being devoted to anti-drone drones.

Regulating these potential battles will pose a political nightmare. Ownership and use of drones is unlikely to be limited to businesses and organizations. Indeed, individual citizens can argue that a drone is needed for security of their homes and properties; Second Amendment defenders will assert that a small drone falls within the category of the right to bear arms. On what basis will elected officials—who are afraid to ban assault weapons—forbid anyone access to a drone?

There is a third and somewhat disconcerting issue. Drone advocates generally eschew the word. They prefer the antiseptic acronym UAVs, short for "unmanned aerial vehicles." The derivation of "drone" is uncertain. A droning sound is monotonous, dull and relentless. Here is a case of onomatopoeia. To grumble that the politician or philosophy teacher just "drooooonnnned" conveys by its very sound the meaning of the word. Early technological drones had a humming sound, though researchers continue to minimize it. A drone also refers to a male bee, who is generally lazy and lives off the work of others.

The first military drones were largely used for target practice to test the accuracy of new weapons. Perhaps today's advocates are also living off the work of their flying gadgets. Whether drones in everyday life contribute to the public good is a gamble taken without significant public discussion. One popular science magazine declares that the drone invasion has already begun, with the only question being how citizens are preparing for it.

Recent interviews and photos of advocates often depict a man cradling a remote control while gazing admiringly at his drone. He talks only of the money he can make from drones if the government, and presumably anyone else, does not interfere. He seems oblivious to the darker possibilities that endanger his fellow citizens. His is one of the faces leading this forthcoming invasion.

Farewell to Privacy?

"Can we say then ... that the general economy of power in our societies is becoming a domain of security?" —*Michel Foucault, 1978*

In 1791, the Fourth Amendment—sanctifying what we now call the human right to privacy—became part of the Bill of Rights. Barely had the ink of the signatures dried when it was already threatened by government. Congress immediately planned to take a census of the newly established country's population, only to be met by numerous citizens resisting officials poking their heads onto their property and asking about their children, size of home, how many males and females were over the age of 16.

More than two centuries later, the right to privacy continues to be threatened and violated. While the focus has changed from physical space and home life to information and data about everyone's behavior and contacts, invasion of privacy might be the only government action that enjoys ongoing bipartisan support. It hardly matters whether the president is Republican or Democrat, or whether Congress is run by conservatives or liberals, as they always find reasons to suspect and spy on their own citizens.

The threat to the Fourth Amendment is fueled by two sources: rapid advances in technology and insidious policies masked by incessant cheers about serving the public good. One early case involved the secrecy of personal mail, which Benjamin Franklin tried to guarantee for all users of his postal system. Yet governments invariably asserted their authority to open up politically rebellious missives or morally corrupting materials.

In the 1880s, New Yorker Anthony Comstock led an anti-vice movement demanding the government manipulate all personal mails to identify and seize sexual aids and contraceptives, as well as obscene pictures and writings. Imagine if Comstock were reincarnated amid today's ubiquitous obscenities.

Inventions of the telegraph and telephone surely speeded and expanded the scope of communication, opening the world for innumerable people. But their everyday use readily enabled the invasion of personal privacy. Current social media are drastic extensions of those inventions.

Advocates of security claim that the right of privacy can be excessive. Surely, they contend, it is for the public good that our governments need to suspend privacy rights in order to catch criminals, hackers, spies, terrorists, pedophiles, traitors, immigrants and innumerable social miscreants. And in the name of the common good, governments are also watching who exercises, drinks a large soda, navigates social media, has healthy sex or eats fatty foods.

Such advocacy has become blind to the excessive emphasis on security. Its proponents refuse to specify limits and at what point personal or group privacy cannot be violated. This bipartisan refusal to protect the Fourth Amendment reveals how governments belittle the fact that privacy is central to each citizen's chance for a life of liberty, equality and the pursuit of happiness.

There are several reasons behind security's prominence. First, security is big business. Shopping malls, museums, college campuses, gated communities, airports, stadiums, and now elementary schools and urban marathons devote considerable budgets to guards, computer experts and surveillance gadgets. Second, security is easier to promote than privacy. By its nature, private life is unannounced. We quietly respect one another's personal lives. Security, by contrast, is visible. Fences, border controls, police and alarm systems are among the mechanisms to show that governments are securing our safety.

In addition, the rhetoric behind security thrives on inflammatory and hyperbolic rhetoric. Every mishap becomes a crisis; we must prepare for a war on this or that; everyone is a potential criminal or terrorist. Third, science and security are veritable soulmates. The technology to extend security rather than protect privacy is more effective and available to governments, but also to other institutions and businesses.

Consider two inventions that will likely enter our daily lives within the next decade. Drones, already a chief weapon in recent wars, are being marketed to governments as well as savvy and ambitious interest groups. These unmanned flying machines can trace the movements of all types of citizens. The state of Texas is already using drones against Mexican immigrants; state police have resorted to their use; and PETA activists are seeking affordable drones to identify poachers and illegal hunters. Last year a tiny, nearly invisible "electronic hummingbird" was selected as one of the year's top 100 inventions. Equipped with a nano-camera, it can survey the minutest motions of any target. When its price drops and efficiency improves, anyone with a remote will be able keep a gaze on vagabonds, voluptuous teens, suspicious spouses, slothful employees, even the neighborhood party one was not invited to.

It is understandable that many commentators believe 9/11 has radically altered our attitudes towards the tenets of the Fourth Amendment. To the contrary, the last 10 years have been a continuation of—not an exception to—the ongoing struggle between privacy and security. Without resistance across the political spectrum, the onslaught upon the basic human right of privacy will continue to erode a key component of democracy and the good life.

Does Watson put our Future in Jeopardy?

Woe to those who, to the very end, insist on regulating the movement that surpasses them with the narrow mind of the mechanic who changes a tire.
—Georges Bataille, The Accursed Share

Watson, an IBM-designed computer, just defeated two of "Jeopardy's" best players. While this is not the first time a computer beat humans in a game — Deep Blue topped a chess champion several years ago — Watson's victory is striking. Before a national audience, computer intelligence outdid its human creator and adversary in speed and memory. And it did so by displaying new skills in detecting the nuances of language and performing creative "mental" maneuvers. To only hear the game, Watson seemed humanlike.

Much more is to come. Watson is already being sought to assist hospital doctors and staff with advising on medical databases and informing patients. Genetic counseling and even marital advice might soon be next. Some ardent advocates of artificial intelligence (AI), such as members of the Singularity movement, emphasize the larger leap: Within 30 years, the linkage of human consciousness, brains and silicon chips will be so accomplished that an individual might envision "living" (whether in a continually regenerating body or in disembodied form that preserves the mind) for eons. Immortality beckons from the horizons again.

This cannot be welcome news from Earth's perspective. It likely views humans as houseguests who have overstayed their welcome. We raid the refrigerator, leave our dirty clothes wherever we go, and routinely terrorize the other inhabitants. If population experts are accurate, in 2045 there will be 9 billion human beings on the planet; that is the same year Singularity members expect Watson and its offspring will triumph as the most intelligent species.

A utopian dream or dystopian nightmare? In evolutionary terms, there is no reason to assume the human mind represents a final pinnacle. Just as some species are displaced by others with greater speed, strength or beauty, so too could humans yield to more intelligent beings. Curiously, AI supporters assume a smooth evolutionary shift, as if the new species will gratefully serve its human designers. But evolution also involves struggle and conflict. With energy resources and living space becoming ever scarcer, the future Watsons of the world might no longer be content just to defeat humans in games of memory and speed.

This longing for immortality is one of the most enduring of human pursuits. Since our supposed exile from paradise, humans have sought magical elixirs, exotic animal organs, perfect climates and cryogenic caskets to extend their lives indefinitely. Current efforts rely on the possibility that consciousness lies in our brain — the original computer — whose synapses and neurons can be transferred to silicon chips and nanotechnology databases.

But human consciousness is more than the knowledge stored in our brain. A child learns the world through the touch in his or her fingers. Our ears intuitively distinguish the harmonies of a Bach concerto from the cacophonies of a committee meeting. Delicate sensors of the tongue inform the wine drinker of a rare find or an overpriced bottle. The skin immediately reacts to a caring touch or an unwanted grasp.

Neurocardiologists now claim that the heart itself alerts us to the approach of a lover or the presence of a danger. These are not just bits of information but a body of knowledge that comprises the human self. One English biologist, Aubrey de Grey, seems unfazed by such observations. A Singularity enthusiast, he believes that human bodies and brains can be likened to antique cars. He would replace aging or damaged parts with updated or regenerative versions.

Yet we do not experience one another as a collection of interchangeable parts. Though often indefinable, there is something irreplaceable in a living creature. To ignore that in search of immortality is a movement that will always surpass and undermine human existence. Woe to those who conclude that this search amounts to little more than changing a tire.

Garbage In, Garbage Out

"Mankind is ... a manifold opening of the possibilities of growth and an infinite capacity for wasteful consumption." —Georges Bataille (1967)

There is something distinctly human about trash. Zoologists and entomologists have found many connections between humans and animal behavior, primate psychology, even the DNA of fruit flies. So far, though, there is no evidence that hordes of bees, colonies of ants or herds of elephants are endangered by their own junk. Only human civilizations pose such a threat to themselves.

What to do about our garbage is a problem that has vexed Baltimore at the highest levels of government in recent months. Soon city residents will learn to live with their trash a couple of extra days, now that Mayor Sheila Dixon and the City Council have decided to reduce trash removal to once a week. The outcry has been widespread, as if the city will soon be swallowed up by rats, raccoons and infectious bacteria. Such scenarios are far-fetched, though the nuisance factor is undeniable.

It is dubious that this policy will have any substantive effect on the municipal budget. The $7 million to be saved will easily diminish when the city begins increasing its inspections and enforcement of the new law. With more recycling dates, opportunities for trash scofflaws will be plentiful and tempting. Anyone hosting a backyard crab feast on a summer weekend is unlikely to tolerate the stench of discarded shells for more than a day, law or no law.

Nonetheless, this policy could be a cultural bellwether. After all, trash is one of humanity's defining characteristics. Estimates vary, but a typical urban resident produces about five times his body weight in refuse annually. This is due not only to our immense consumption but also the bags, bubble wraps, Styrofoam blocks and cardboard   boxes that protect the things we buy. Electronic gadgets are so tightly packaged that even the nimblest fingers   and most patient minds can face a headache-inducing venture. To grab an aspirin for the headache means to penetrate a box, twist off cap and sealed label - more future offerings to our garbage heap.

Awash in trash, we use it as noun, verb and adjective. Trash talking can involve intimidation, braggadocio or simple rubbish. Rowdies and college students on spring break are known for trashing a room or locale. To call someone trashy is to question his or her moral standing or personal hygiene. And none of us likes to be treated as trash, whether by a grumpy boss or snobby neighbor.

There is a branch in the social sciences called garbology. Its research relies on the principle that many of our habits and secrets can be found in wastebaskets and trash cans. Discarded items can open a window to someone's finances, love life, medical needs and family foibles, as well as indulgences and bad habits.

Trash might be civilization's most lasting accomplishment. More than sacred texts, beautiful temples and monuments, or great works of art and music, man-made plastic promises to survive nuclear wars and global warming. According to David Ferris, a writer for Sierra magazine, scientists are learning that minute elements of plastic seem never to completely disintegrate. Nurdles, the basic components of plastic, are now found in the digestive systems of fish, in the nests of hermit crabs, in the excrement of fur seals. Should aliens descend upon this planet in a millennium or two, they will infer that an intelligent species once inhabited the place - not from such as evidence as museums and libraries, but from nurdles sparkling in dung heaps and animal dwellings.

Anthropologists note that one of the more endearing social lubricants is the gift. The ritual of potlatch - periodic sharing of meals and valuables - is often highlighted because reciprocity among different individuals is expected and encouraged. The same cannot be said of trash. Trash involves hierarchy, not circularity. Someone lower on the social order handles the bulk of it; the poorest of the poor live amid the refuse of the rich. If residents volunteered to take turns and haul each other's garbage cans to a common corner, trucks could save considerable time from negotiating the narrow alleys. And we could easily have trash pickups twice a week.

But trash is a tricky business. We don't want our neighbors sneaking a peek into our secret lives (or possibly stealing our identities). And we certainly don't want to expose our own infinite capacity for wasteful consumption.

The Weapons of Greatness

But not to perish of internal distress and uncertainty when one inflicts great suffering and hears the cry of this suffering—that is great, that belongs to greatness. —Nietzsche

When a tornado cuts a swath through a town, it levels the buildings in minutes. Earthquakes will rip asunder entire cities in less than an hour. Volcanoes can bury villages in a day or two. As long as humans have lived on this earth, they have been subject to large-scale and rapid forms of devastation—by the forces of nature.

Awed by this immense power, humans have emulated nature's forces by inventing their own quick and extensive methods of devastation. They are referred to as weapons of mass destruction. Having them and reaping benefits from their threats and actual uses of them are testimony to one's greatness. In earlier times these inventions were deployed by engulfing enemies in flames, exploding their defenses with dynamite or cannon balls, dropping grenades with the rapidity of machine guns, or burning their lungs with mustard gas. In the last century the potential for destruction has dared the limits of our imagination. Not only can civilizations surpass the power of volcanoes and earthquakes, they now are able to simulate the explosive energies of the sun and incinerate whole populations in little more than a blink of any eye. They have rivaled the forces of a malevolent deity.

In this light, it is strange that those who led the debates prior to the invasion of Iraq included the United States, Britain, France,

China, Russia, and Germany. Think of countries that have engaged in weapons of mass destruction, and these six are among the top candidates for greatness. Britain's firebombing of Dresden and massacre of peaceful marchers in India,

Germany's deployment of mustard gas in Ypres and Kyclon B in its gas chambers, and America's release of napalm and Agent Orange in Vietnam form only a partial list.

Russia (as the former Soviet Union) and China have used their tools of devastation on neighboring peoples and millions of their own. Britain and France, as well as any country with colonies, required weapons of mass destruction to efficiently control natives in faraway lands. Although the United States and France spare their citizens additional taxes, this is achieved by trafficking weaponry to numerous armies throughout the world. Each of these countries, of course, sought or has the trigger to a nuclear bomb. (So far, only one has pulled the trigger.) In other words, each has blood dropping from its hands.

Yet to acquire greatness demands considerable bloodletting. It is not enough to give the world Bach, Edison, Tchaikovsky, Picasso, Shakespeare or Confucius. Works of beauty or creativity might inspire the awe of love, but not the awe of fear. Political greatness seeks the latter.

Saddam Hussein, who ascended to power by torturing the executing fellow Iraqis, must realize this. While those debating his future are not personally brutal, this comparison is probably futile. For this war with Iraq is more than a battle between George Bush and his lackeys versus the forces of evil and their acolytes. It transcends the quest for cheap oil or United Nations accords.

The current debate is among powers of greatness and whether they will tolerate another aspiring power. This debate does not require consistency of principle or beliefs. One decade UN council members call Hussein an ally, the next they call for his exile or death. Over 250,000 soldiers have attacked Iraq, though North Korea poses a greater nuclear threat.

Not only are the powers of greatness capricious, their debates lack earnestness. Speculating on the nature of future wars, British physicist David Langford pointed out that atom bombs were given names such as Little Boy, Grand Slam and Davy Crockett. Today, euphemisms such as "smart bombs" or "precision missiles" conceal the fact that this invasion of Iraq is not only aimed at one of Saddam's palaces, but will likely obliterate many Iraqi civilians.

The likelihood of this obliteration, however, seems not to cause distress for today's worldly powers. As Nietzsche observes, they did not reach greatness through empathy, but by turning a deaf ear to the cries of suffering their greatness produces.

A City in Crisis? In Chaos?

At first I did not take the smoke seriously. Trains pulling through Mount Royal Station leave an occasional mark in the air. Television crews were arriving, but they and their offspring pop up anywhere. So when firemen quietly but quickly began alerting local residents, merchants, and pedestrians of possible poisons in the air, I sensed something urgent was happening in Baltimore.

Typically, my worry was the mile-long trek home. For Baltimore residents, that meant avoiding the jams generated by commuters from nearby counties. While they anxiously sought for the magic passage to the JFX, city residents knew, for example, that going north on Eutaw Street to Druid Hill was the way out.

To those living near Mount Royal Station (and downtown, as it turned out), things were more precarious. Should they leave their homes or apartments? How drastic was the potential hazard? From the eyes of television, however, people who lived closest to the sources of the train wreck were given a cold shoulder. Instead, the focus was on all those who were passing through—not in their tattered clothes carrying all they own on their backs, as of earlier nomads, but in their mobiles stocked with cushioned seats and climate control buttons.

The local networks warmly embraced commuters, patrons of a baseball team, and the tourists who never venture past the Inner Harbor. Trying to "get personal" meant: an interview with the sorrowful family from Columbia or White Marsh who could not see the O's, a quick survey if the Hooters or ESPN Zone lost money for a day or two, or a screen flush with diagrams of roads blocked and transportation systems altered that might affect tomorrow's commute.

To highlight these possible horrors, local stations led with headlines about a city in crisis or chaos.

Ignorance? False advertisement? Anti-urban hype?

Those with a sense of Baltimore history would answer yes. Hearing of a city in chaos, they recall riots, bloodshed, destruction, and conflicting passions. Picture Baltimore after the 1968 assassination of Martin Luther King, Jr. Imagine the city when a large chunk of its downtown burned down in the Fire of 1904. Or study how a racially progressing Baltimore of the 1830's transformed into polarized neighborhoods a decade later, bringing about fiery battles among freed slaves, immigrant Irish and Germans, and conniving entrepreneurs.

The train wreck of 2001 pales in comparison.

Of course it could have been worse—never underestimate luck or fortune. Yet this was unknown by television figures who stare at the station's computers and then feverishly read from them to the audience, as if filing a report from the trenches.

Given the stations' expensive and modern gadgetry, one might assume that television would find compelling such scenes as city parents putting their children asleep or friends inquiring about the safety of their neighbors in a climate that could resemble chemical warfare. Viewers could then discover how people in the city face a possible crisis among the vagaries of urban life. Irresponsibly, however, the television networks decided that the catastrophe of not seeing Cal one more time or missing the Aquarium's latest shark exhibit spoke of a city already in chaos. To the contrary. With police and fire departments giving immense attention to the train accident, Baltimore was in anything but chaos. No stores were burning, no curfew was ordered, and no National Guard was called in. At least the train accident in the secret tunnel reminded or taught many of us how essential Baltimore is to life in Maryland and in the country.

This lesson should be remembered during the next election campaign, when politicians curry the favors of voters by protesting against additional support for Baltimore. Or, displaying rare nerve, will they ask the commuters from Columbia or White Marsh if they would rather have freight trains full of hazardous materials regularly passing the Pavilion or running parallel to The Avenue?

Needlepark Zoo

Needlepark, Switzerland's experiment to control AIDS, has closed down. It was from the start a strange ambition: spotlessly clean Zurich handing out sterile needles to contaminated citizens. In a country whose quality-of-life index ranks highest in the world, even admitting the need for such an experiment must have been difficult.

What resulted was part zoo, part freak show. Imagine taking a stroll through Baltimore's Inner Harbor. You then detour up to Federal Hill for a panoramic view of the city. Instead you are treated to a quite different spectacle. You see a lad, wearing an Orioles cap, injecting his friend with heroin. The friend is too far gone to find a usable vein.

You turn away, only to spot a neighbor's daughter in a Hammerjacks T-shirt, numb and huddled on a nearby bench. A man patiently talks to her. Later you learn that the man was either a private investigator, hired by the girl's parents to retrieve her, or a pimp who offers a better deal. That was Needlepark.

It also resembled a human observatory. Everyone was looking or being looked at. Medical aides kept an eye on possible overdoses. Pedestrians watched out for dazed and stumbling addicts on a high. Pushers and addicts were in mutual searches for a sale. And tourists nervously let their cameras do the seeing.

Like a zoo, Needlepark was full of gazes containing a mixed message: a sense of utter detachment among the denizens with an eerie feeling that we still had some connection.

Needlepark was not only a spectacle. It was an attempt in social policy, one that American cities have considered emulating. With the fear of AIDS rapidly spreading, particularly through needles, urban and medical officials were eager to hear about the merits of the Swiss experiment. Yet the novelty of the experiment probably had too little time to be proved successful or not.

Still, most will conclude that it was a failure, thus keeping Americans as well as the Swiss and the world guessing about dealing with the spread of AIDS. Others might disagree. Perhaps, they argue, American ingenuity can correct the mistakes of the Swiss.

That ingenuity, though, will have to accomplish the following: Persuade all of Baltimore's addicts to come to Federal Hill, or some centrally located area, without fear of arrest, exchange dirty needles for clean ones, inject their heroin two blocks from Baltimore's main tourist attraction, and then pray that no one finds it very strange, or ugly.

Needle park was strange. It could show you old schoolmates walking about with blood trickling down their necks, or needles dangling from the back of their knees. It would have you glancing at half-naked lovers, oblivious to the dying surrounding them. It might catch you staring at a rescue of an overdose.

Suppose, then, that an expert panel could convince us that a properly administered Needlepark could reduce the spread of AIDS. How many of us are willing to accept the spectacle? The Geraldo show is one thing, but would we let Federal Hill become a public freak show? Who says that our sons and daughters may parade about in a human zoo?

Baltimore's Foolish Indy Car Fantasy

Corporation, n. An ingenious device for obtaining individual profit without individual responsibility.
—Ambrose Bierce, The Devil's Dictionary

Big-time car racing, now among the most popular spectator sports, is coming to Baltimore.

If local officials and business leaders have their way, a Grand Prix event will be held in the city as early as August 2011. It is expected to draw more than 100,000 visitors to the city for a long weekend, bringing in hundreds of millions of dollars. (Presumably, they have never been in downtown Baltimore during a sweltering August heat wave.)

According to organizers, these visitors will gladly spend $2,000 for a three-day weekend that revolves around watching dozens of cars go endlessly around the same track, burned rubber sifting through the air, ethanol fumes seeping into spectators' lungs, fiery accidents grabbing their eyes, and dedicated fans swilling as much beer as humanly possible.

And Baltimore City, they audaciously claim, will profit. This claim is specious. The enduring promise of major short- term sporting events - that they generate increased jobs and significant tax revenue - has yet to be proven. Most of the jobs are temporary and without benefits. The tax revenue is couched in terms of contingency (expected attendance, weather, media coverage), so profits for the city are at best a vague projection.

Also disturbing is that city residents are not addressing the environmental aspects of this event. They seem oblivious to the fact that car racing is a nature-lover's nightmare. Race cars average 3 to 5 miles per gallon, depending on weather, speed, curves and surface of the track. During a three- to four-hour race, drivers waste considerable rubber, going through five or six sets of tires. For ecologists, the so-called carbon footprint left by the Grand Prix is disastrous.

Then there is the gas-guzzling entourage. Like rock stars, drivers travel in their own luxury motor homes. A truck carries two cars. And a third van carries the memorabilia for marketing sponsorships, such as breweries and oil companies. Downtown traffic, already congested, will be a logjam for days as organizers set up stands and prepare the roads.

Jay Davidson, a corporate lawyer, is one of the chief proponents of this event. He understandably emphasizes that restaurants, hotels and businesses will benefit greatly from a Baltimore Grand Prix. He is also understandably quiet about how this will benefit mostly business owners and not the hundreds of thousands of citizens residing outside the five downtown communities that are guaranteed $100,000 annually from the race's organizers - ostensibly for community development but more likely to purchase community approval.

Finally, there is a side effect ignored by organizers and city officials. Race car fans, like most sports fans, imitate what they admire. When kids see Kobe Bryant make a twisting lay-up or Venus Williams crush a marvelous return, they rush outside and try the same. When Adelaide, Australia, hosted its first Grand Prix in 1986, there was a sudden spike in traffic accidents.

Fueled by a case of beer, the temptation to emulate their idols will be hard for some Grand Prix spectators to resist, as they hop in their cars and zip across Pratt Street at 90 mph, swerve between two MTA buses at 110 mph, then dart onto the JFX at 160 mph.

The odds that this event will benefit Baltimore are a virtual coin toss. If it goes well, corporate leaders can boast. If not, then, as Ambrose Bierce anticipated long ago, someone else will get the blame.

4
Liberal or Libertarian?

Introduction

How strange that liberal and libertarian share the same Latin root for "freedom." The term "liberty" has been part of many political and revolutionary slogans, including Patrick Henry's famed "Give me liberty or give me death!" If we ask ten liberals and ten libertarians which politicians they voted for, however, they would unlikely reflect their etymological kinship.

Libertarians tend to be staunch defenders of individual freedoms and the Bill of Rights. For them freedom of speech and assembly are fundamental strengths of a democratic society, so they worry that a large government weakens or undermines these strengths. If you allow the fiery speech of enraged communists, then you also have to put up with the nasty words of white supremacists. Libertarians assume that adults can be entrusted to make informed decisions about their personal lives without the intrusive and paternalistic guidance of elected officials. Hence their emphasis on individual freedoms within the constraints of political society.

Liberals, on the other hand, tend to focus on freedom as opportunity. Given the various inequalities among citizens, liberals think governments (and citizens) have a responsibility to provide better chances (or erase obstacles to) for people to have more opportunities and options in life. Often liberal causes get mocked when they fret over the policies about junk food or public restrooms. These minor issues unfortunately obscure how many liberal causes—such as civil rights for blacks, women and gays—have enhanced the opportunities and freedoms for millions of Americans over the last sixty years.

This divide between liberals and libertarians is unfortunate, since they actually have much in common. Though for different reasons sometimes, both sides tend to support the legalization of marijuana and abortion, denounce capital punishment and the growth of the prison population, offer compassion to immigrants and welcome the open integration of gays and lesbians into everyday life. Curiously, when I critique a liberal position, liberals accuse me of being a conservative. When I critique a libertarian position, I'm considered another busy-body liberal. This commonality and tension have guided the following pieces.

To highlight my own ambivalence, the essays are presented in chronological sequence, starting with the most recent.

The Essays

On the second or third Sunday of January, for the longest time there has been a celebration of the Lee/Jackson statue in Wyman Park, fifty yards from the Baltimore Museum of Art. Men and women would appear in Civil War regalia, playing trumpets and drums, singing Dixie, and offering short speeches to recognize the birth date of Robert E. Lee and the legacy of the South. They never talked about race or slavery, only some imaginary return to the 1890s of America. As I live two blocks away, I saw this event often. After the ceremony, they would go to a hall on Hopkins campus for refreshments.

To me, the celebrants were a bunch of eccentrics to be enjoyed and not taken seriously. Soon they were taken seriously as purveyors of racism and slavery. They were blocked by protestors during a recent commemoration. I stopped by and was caught off guard.

Someone handed me a flyer and I responded that I do not support liberal fascism. Within a minute or two, another protestor confronted me with a camera, several inches from my face. When I objected, he and several others insisted they had a right to be as close to my face as they want, since this was public property.

It was quite intimidating, as they were baiting me to smash the camera. The one holding the camera followed me around, finally asking if I get sexually aroused when I utter 'liberal fascism'". The Sun's editor recommended we delete that point, not out of censorship, but because it would need an extra paragraph or two to provide the proper context. And my essay was already over 700 words. The essay did get me invited for an interview with a local radio station. Oddly, nearly all the e-mails sent to me were kind and gracious for challenging this virulent in-your-face form of liberalism, whereas the Sun's on-line comments site most wondered if I was a racist.

The treatment and status of animals draw a wide range of attitudes throughout the world. To protect the lives and well-being of animals, a number of advocates argue that rights and personhood should be ascribed to animals, particularly those held captive in zoos, circuses and aquariums.

My daughter has probably appreciated animals more than human beings most of her life. When she was ten, we watched Alfred Hitchcock's movie "The Birds," where thousands of ravens and starlings are fiercely attacking a family holed up in a small beach house. She was rooting for the feathered creatures. When my son was six years old, he discovered a dead bird in the back yard (maybe murdered by our cat) and insisted we bury the little guy. He said a brief prayer on the bird's behalf. My kids' attitudes were not based on rights or personhood, but compassion for non-human living creatures. Their early experiences partly guided this essay.

There is an element of bad faith in my commenting on commencement speakers. I try to avoid commencement ceremonies and have never attended one for my own college degrees. I respect individuals who, unlike me, speak well before an audience of hundreds or thousands of people. What struck my attention here was how both liberals and conservatives were engaging in the battle of approving or rejecting commencement speakers. Yet many of the speakers were already invited in compliance with conventional selection criteria.

The saddest example was Condaleeza Rice. She's an accomplished, bright and thoughtful human being. She had the potential for a career in playing the piano, but decided on other goals. To rescind her invitation because she worked for a president you did not like seemed to me a current example of a mini-inquisition.

The essay on liberal intolerance evokes my most libertarian instincts. Much of what Benjamin Carson says about social issues is amusing or ill-informed. It is so easy for us liberals to mock Carson's comment about gays, taxes, and parental discipline. Unfortunately, mocking him is a very flimsy response. When Carson cites the Bible or alleged authorities on child rearing, his critics should specify where he is mistaken about sacred texts or current experts. Instead, they emphasize his silly miscues while ignoring the fact that millions of Americans like him.

One of my students, conscientious and hard-working, told me that she had numerous brain operations as a child. The surgeon was Ben Carson. If you read some of his reflections as a doctor, Carson says the most difficult task is not with the child, but telling the parents the brain surgery is so delicate that they might not see their child alive again. He had this encounter with hundreds of parents. Regardless of his attempts at social commentary, Benjamin Carson has a remarkable record when responding to other humans in life and death situations. Maybe we liberals can cut him some slack while our libertarian side grants his right to speak.

Since the publication of Allan Bloom's *Closing of the American Mind* conservatives have berated higher education as a bastion of liberalism. This is evident in the courses taught, professors' public views about current controversies, even departmental disputes about which faculty to hire or promote. A number of professors admit that they do not convey their conservative positions until they have been accepted for a position or granted tenure.

This backlash is a bit myopic. When conservatives whine about academic liberalism they somehow forget that higher education is run very much like a big business. Students are considered customers or consumers of education. College presidents are referred to as CEOs, and they earn substantial salaries, anywhere from $400,000 to over $1,00,000. Meanwhile, many universities rely on adjuncts—paid piecemeal wages with no benefits—to teach many of their courses. Perhaps there are a disproportionate number of liberal professors in academe, but this is easily outweighed by the dominance of corporate culture in higher education.

Liberals and libertarians lament our inability to resolve the difficulty of preventing suffering as people face terminable illnesses and diseases. The slogans overwhelming the assisted suicide disputes are quite familiar: Don't play God; death with dignity; we put horses and dogs out of their misery; there's always hope.

This essay was initiated by the death of a very kind neighbor, Jack. I met his sons and one of them, a lawyer, twice played Santa Claus for my two children when they were still toddlers. With Jack's illness worsening, he was taken to the emergency room one night, where medical people declared him to be dead and contacted the sons, who then relayed the sad news to family and friends. The hospital officials soon called back to say there was a mistake. The father was still living, but barely. The next morning the father died. The sons had grounds for a law suit but did not pursue that option. The one who played Santa Claus later told me that there was no legal culpability among the medical people who tried their best—it was moral confusion over how to treat those who are near death.

For conservatives and libertarians who insist that academe is a hotspot for socialist experiments and egalitarian utopias, they might investigate the business of textbooks. (Disclosure, I published one.) Stop by a local book store and you will not find them on display. Textbooks are bulky, unwieldy and expensive. You would not go to the beach or a public park and take a textbook for pleasant reading. Moreover, courses that require textbooks rarely cover the entire material, for they are often created to appeal to three or four different ways of teaching a basic course. Many college anthologies contain eighty to one hundred selections. For a fifteen week course that meets three times a week, that could mean at most forty five selections are read or discussed. But the eighty to one hundred selections give instructors options to focus on historical materials, recurring disputes, or thematic issues. Some textbooks in the sciences and businesses cost over $200. Given the market of used textbooks, second and third editions become more pressing to enhance the publisher's (and editors) chances for sustained profits.

The essay on secularism was my rejoinder to Crispin Sartwell's op-ed attack on religious traditions and believers. Here William Connolly's *Why I am not a Secularist* lies in the background. Connolly's critique of secularists was not based on any personal commitment to religious beliefs. I've read several of Connolly's books. It is possible he is an agnostic or atheist, though he clearly has a spiritual side when it comes to nature, justice and friendship. Regardless, he claims that many secularists underestimate the power of religion and human beings' willingness to believe in something that is not founded or supported in science, technology, capitalism or enlightenment. And secularism, socialist or libertarian, offers few meaningful options to the good life as envisioned by religious believers. Admittedly, my 700 word essay barely scratches the surface in light of Connolly's scholarly treatise.

In Owings Mills, a suburb of Baltimore, two brothers admitted to shooting three unarmed men, one fatally. They owned a cement factory that was broken into a couple of times. So one night they stayed at the factory with their loaded guns. Sure enough, three intruders arrived in the middle of the night and the two brothers were ready. They pleaded self-defense and won.

As libertarians are staunch supporters of the Bill of Rights, including the 2nd (right to bear arms) and the 4th (the right not to have one's own property seized or invaded), they would likely agree with the jury's "not guilty" verdict. Liberals are well-known for their willingness to weaken the right to own guns and would likely find it abhorrent that shooting three unarmed men goes with no punishment. Vigilante justice? Actually, some liberals agreed with the verdict.

As a footnote, I later received a personal letter from a woman who lived near the factory. She wrote that with the shooting and police sirens, she and several neighbors woke up and checked the scene of the crime. She claimed that the man who eventually died was wounded for several hours and pleaded with the brothers to call an ambulance. They did not.

Choosing to die on your own terms is a theme addressed since Plato and Seneca. For them the issue wasn't that we own our bodies and lives and should have a right to make the key decisions. Rather, the issue was freedom and not being a slave to someone else's dictate over the circumstances of our dying.

What sparked this essay was the suicide of a woman in her mid-twenties. She was Jewish, not very popular with guys, and considerably shy. She fell in love with a young Christian man and they wanted to marry. Her parents nixed it, insisting that husband is one who practices the Jewish faith. The whole story just seemed very sad and tragic, but it struck a nerve about the right to commit suicide. I introduced the argument to an ethics class and a student in her late twenties raised her hand. Her husband had committed suicide several years before, leaving behind a widow, two youngsters and no explanation. Whatever right one might have to commit suicide does not supersede the lasting and indescribable damage done to others when exercising that right. I have yet to find a suitable response to this student.

My run-in with liberal fascists

For Rob and Laurie

There is a specter haunting American politics. It shows up everywhere from college campuses to city parks. It is belligerent, relentless and techno-savvy. It is liberal fascism, and I recently got a close-up view.

Taking a weekend walk in Baltimore, I unexpectedly met protesters in front of the Robert E. Lee and Thomas J. "Stonewall" Jackson Monument in the Wyman Park Dell. One walked up and offered me a leaflet. "No thanks," I said, "I don't support liberal fascism." Just a flippancy on my part, but it turns out to have been quite a mistake.

Suddenly a young man appeared before me, with a camera six inches from my face. I asked what he was doing and why he neglected to seek my permission to be photographed. He ignored my request to leave, got closer and launched into a speech about his First Amendment rights. The camera lens almost touched my eyeglasses; I brushed it away, and the backlash was instant.

Other protesters surrounded me. One carried a placard about ending white supremacy. I reached for it to help block the harassing camera. She pulled the placard away. Both protesters denied that a camera six inches from someone's face poses any threat. Sensing this to be a futile visit, I inched away. They continued to stalk me. Nearby protesters from a local Quaker congregation did nothing to intervene.

At the scene was a reporter wrapping up his assignment. With several protesters next to me, I asked whether it is a common practice and courtesy to seek permission from persons before taking their picture. He nods yes. Regardless, says a woman protester, her group has a right to confront me while on public grounds. I wonder if she would hold that view should she walk home one evening with a strange man keeping pace beside her while incessantly holding his iPhone before her eyes.

Another protester approached me with a predictable accusation: racism. How a simple request to remove a protester's camera from my face is racist stretches common logic. One might speculate that if the protesters were serious about their slogans, they would be working in the danger zones of western Baltimore rather than pacing about in the safe environs of a public park demonstrating against the losing side of a 150-year-old war.

The term fascism derives from an Italian word meaning "group, bundle or assemblage." It was drawn from an Aesop fable about single sticks being weak, while a bunch of sticks becomes quite strong. Fascism survives by adopting a herd's ethos on driving out alleged apostates. It thrives with a Manichaean attitude that you are either with us or against us. Like the witch hunters and Klansmen before them, fascists energize their forces to suspend a basic respect for others while insisting on their own rights and privileges.

Usually fascism is linked with right-wing tyrants and religious zealots. What distinguishes liberal fascism is outrage masked by humanitarian words. Liberal fascists promote tolerance while quashing disagreement. They speak of compassion yet do not hesitate to humiliate a stranger.

They bait and taunt you with insults before their gang, but never one to one. Liberal fascists are among the most vociferous bullies of today's politics.

After my experience in Baltimore, my son—who is adept with social media—took a walk to the same locale. Soon protesters approached and asked him questions. One accused him of white privilege and put a camera to his face. He informs me that they dare you to lose your patience or temper so they could immediately record and distribute the outburst on social media. Good thing I remained calm.

Many liberals have been charging Republican presidential candidate Donald Trump with fascist proclivities. If this brief scene in Baltimore is typical, the charge is akin to calling the kettle black. These protesters emulated fascist habits anchored by insults, bullying and distortion.

It does not matter to them that I have supported many liberal ideas since long before they were born. It does not matter to them that I went to North Carolina to research and publish a story on how a college basketball team sparked racial integration in Winston-Salem. Facts do not matter to them—only surges of self-righteousness and momentary pleasures of intimidating another human being.

My flippant rejoinder that started all this was ironically prophetic. These protesters did turn out to be liberal fascists. Without inquiry, they simply bundled up—like the sticks in an Aesop fable—to berate and intimidate a solitary pedestrian hoping to enjoy some of the lovely sights of Baltimore.

Are Animals People too?

*"We do not regard the animals as moral beings.
But do you suppose the animals regard us as moral
beings?" —Friedrich Nietzsche, Daybreak*

Should mammals be considered persons? There is a growing movement led by animal advocates and legal researchers who answer yes. They have recently brought their case to several state courts claiming certain mammals, such as dolphins and chimpanzees, deserve to be assigned the legal status of personhood.

Skeptics might jest: We will soon announce wedding ceremonies for gorillas, guarantee health insurance for whales, or overthrow pet stores to liberate the enslaved captives. This initial response overlooks the moral gravity presented by such advocacy.

Supporters for animal personhood insist they are riding the coattails of previous groups who have overthrown the status of non-persons. Slaves, women and children once had their freedoms and dignity denied, since they were considered property or inferior underlings. The fight for their basic rights is a precedent for bestowing personhood to non-human yet highly intelligent and sociable mammals. Advocates also promise numerous benefits to mammals once their new rights are established. They will be again free, no longer held captive in zoos, circuses, aquariums and scientific laboratories.

This advocacy is not convincing. Slaves, women and children were eventually deemed to be persons due to their capacity to recognize one another's rights, principles and beliefs. They eventually became, under human law or before God's eye, formally equal to everyone else. Obviously animals have contributed mightily to human well-being. That does not prove they are persons capable of recognizing the rights of others. The same could be said for artificially intelligent machines for which the techno-savvy types debate assigning personhood.

British scholar Mary Midgely notes that "person" comes from Latin meaning mask. She refers not to the costume ball or Halloween mask, but the various dramas a person encounters in human life. As oppressed human beings began participating more freely in private and public domains –drinking at water fountains, voting or pursuing higher education –their status as persons gradually gained legal support. Presumably, animal advocates envision chimpanzees enjoying their newfound autonomy by freely mingling at the shopping mall, cafe or movie theatre.

The prediction that personhood-status will improve the lives of those fortunately designated species is even more specious. Animal advocates point to human rights as their model. Perhaps they have neglected recent news. This year more than 200 Nigerian school girls were kidnapped in a single incident, and the search for them appears inactive. A defenseless airline with travelers and scientists was inexplicably shot down. Civilians on humanitarian missions have been publicly beheaded. Dictatorial regimes, terrorizing their own citizens, are financially propped up by wealthy countries. Having rights does not seem to have helped these innocent persons.

Human rights and personhood have become pawns in a devious international game. According to the Freedom House research group, of 195 independent countries in the world, only 88—fewer than half—are categorized as "free" in terms of respecting citizens' liberties, civic rights and independent media. Meanwhile over 160 countries endorsed one or more of the international treaties for universal rights, suggesting that dozens of countries proclaim on paper to support basic rights but in reality do not. If we cannot guarantee the protection and enjoyment of rights for human persons, on what basis do we expect better results for animals?

In this context, University of Chicago law professor Eric Posner contends that human rights is an outdated ideal, if not counterproductive. The tragedies and cruelties depicting blatant violations of basic rights are fodder for evening news programs. The capacity to violate this ideal without getting caught increases with every new ideology and technology. A country signs off on the treaties in order to deflect potential investigation of its own inhuman practices. By extending personhood to animals, it seems implausible to expect their suffering would be any different than it has been for humans.

This is not to say that animals should be treated as objects or tools directed by the whims of human authority. Rather, the lives of animals and our moral regard for them might be improved in terms of beauty or sacred wonders. We can speak on their behalf in the name of significance to the ecosystem or mirrors of our own natural inclinations—just not in the name of rights and personhood.

Speak not, lest ye be judged

"...You should see that obedient flock who at the mere sign from me will hasten to heap the hot cinders upon the stakes in which we shall burn you for coming to meddle with us." —Fyodor Dostoyevsky, "The Grand Inquisitor" parable within *The Brothers Karamazov.*

Commencement ceremonies are meant for families and friends of the new graduates to celebrate a loved one's move to another stage in life and for the hosting school to celebrate itself and its commitment to education. For students, the exercise is often a dull respite between nights of partying and exchanging farewells.

But for a growing number of people in academia, this ceremony offers the chance to engage in mini-inquisitions of selected keynote speakers—including, this year, former Secretary of State Condoleezza Rice and International Monetary Fund (IMF) head Christine Lagarde. While not as bloody as grand inquisitions, academic inquisitions are otherwise quite similar. Their leaders are as unwavering in their convictions and self-righteousness.

It seems to go something like this: Upon announcement of a keynote speaker, campus activists quickly gather news and rumors in order to publicly denounce the individual. The charges are vague but volatile. When repeated by similarly outraged people (particularly those skilled in social media), the charges sometimes stick and the speakers bow out.

Contrary to principles of modern democracy, inquisitions in general forbid the accused to face their accusers and address the charges. This one-sidedness was obviously reinforced by the tortures and executions of the grand inquisitions. Here the imbalance is assured because the invited speaker tends to gracefully withdraw rather than have the hosts suffer further embarrassment. Not quite the violent death of grand inquisitions, but still an impressive victory for campus inquisitors.

The spate of mini-inquisitions this year is striking. A former chancellor of Berkeley declined to speak after faculty and students of Haverford College complained how Berkeley's police used force on recent Occupy protesters. Ms. Lagarde of the IMF withdrew her acceptance to Smith College's commencement due to allegations that her organization furthered the oppression of women around the world.

Most alarming are the cases of Hirsi Ali and Condoleezza Rice. Ms. Ali, an internationally known women's rights advocate, was invited to speak and receive an honorary doctorate at Brandeis University. She is a harsh critic of Islam, which Brandeis apparently failed to note. Once enlightened by the blogosphere, Brandeis rescinded the degree offer. Ms. Ali observed how women in her native Somalia sacrificed their bodies and souls to preserve family honor. She herself was subject to genital mutilation, as were many girls her age. For Ms. Ali these experiences were central to Muslim tradition. Later her friend Theo van Gogh was assassinated in Amsterdam by a Muslim terrorist angered by van Gogh's artistic perspectives on his religion. Presumably, by banning her, Brandeis sees its Muslim students as incapable of forming their own thoughtful responses to Ms. Ali's criticism.

The mini-inquisition of Condoleezza Rice has a different twist. Here is a woman so bright and multi-talented that she studied to be a concert pianist. She instead became a scholar and award- winning teacher, then served as an advisor and secretary of state in the George W. Bush administration. She accepted a keynote speaker invitation from Rutgers University. Once announced on campus, faculty and students amassed a social media protest to force a change, claiming that her role in the Iraq war represents a crime against humanity. As of today Condoleezza Rice is a free citizen and employed as a distinguished professor while under no legal indictment. Apparently these facts do not upset Rutgers University when one of its own lobbies wild accusations.

Cynics might be correct that inquisitions are part of our historical landscape. Still, places of education have been sanctuaries from the zealotry and self-righteousness that fuel these inquisitions. That these sanctuaries are becoming the breeding grounds for new kinds of inquisition tells young people that free inquiry, critical thinking and democratic discourse apply only to people with whom you agree.

In her memoir Hirsi Ali observed that there are times when "silence becomes an accomplice to injustice." Protesters of commencement invitations are perpetrating a coercive silence upon accomplished individuals. That graduating students and their guests are deprived of the chance to hear these keynote speakers undermines the ideals of public discourse.

In this light, those leading these mini-inquisitions are accomplices to gross injustices.

Liberal intolerance

Liberal media have again shown that they can be just as self-righteous and intolerant as their ardent conservative adversaries.

How else to account for the recent furor over views expressed by a world-renowned pediatric surgeon, neurologist and medical scholar? Baltimore's Dr. Benjamin Carson, an eminent Johns Hopkins Hospital figure long admired by people of all political stripes, including many liberals, is now being derided as a turncoat or doddering fool. His invitation to speak at a Hopkins commencement might be withdrawn.

Upon announcing his impending retirement from medical practice, Dr. Carson has begun to air his concerns over contemporary issues. He has advocated the occasional use of spanking to discipline children and a flat tax for all citizens. At this year's National Prayer Breakfast, with President Barack Obama sitting nearby, Dr. Carson outlined serious reservations with the president's policies on health care. And most contentious has been his assertion that marriage is by definition limited to one man and one woman.

These are fairly common perspectives. When articulated by Dr. Carson, though, liberals seem to have discovered the clay feet of a fallen hero. He has been denounced as a biblical conservative, a believer in antiquated or irrational principles—even an Uncle Tom for Fox News. These ad hominems thwart rather than nourish the democratic dialogue Dr. Carson says he yearns for.

Consider his points. Children have been spanked for centuries. A slap on the hand, for instance, is sometimes the best way parents can convey their disapproval to an unruly toddler.

To label this as "corporal punishment" is an inept response to Dr. Carson's view. As he relies on biblical passages and criticism of Dr. Benjamin Spock's theory of raising children, liberals would be advised to highlight where Dr. Carson has possibly misinterpreted Scripture or Dr. Spock.

Dr. Carson also cites biblical support for a flat tax. Yes, such a position can be easily mocked, as has been done by at least one local pundit. But if liberal pundits took some effort to research rather than offer flippant quips, they would find in Dr. Carson's recent book, "Take the Risk," a more thorough account of his thinking. There he reflects on how many wealthy people he has met who pay very little in taxes. They can elude the IRS by hiding their personal income in arcane corporate shells, loopholes in tax laws, or banks outside the country, such as the Cayman Islands, where they simply avoid taxes altogether. End all those benefits, writes Dr. Carson, and a flat tax would actually make the very wealthy pay more taxes. Again, he may be wrong, but his newfound critics should point out where and how instead of attacking him.

The most vociferous outrage has been over marriage. In a recent interview, Dr. Carson stated that marriage has always been between one man and one woman—presumably, as the wedding vows proclaim, "until death do you part." While this definition is historically misleading, it does preclude marriages between gays or lesbians. Dr. Carson then added that advocates of NAMBLA (an organization promoting sex between men and boys) or bestiality cannot redefine marriage. It was a stupid comment for which he later apologized.

But suppose Dr. Carson meant the following: If we allow gays and lesbians to marry, then on what basis do we accept or deny future proposals for expanding the definition? Perhaps the laws prohibiting siblings will be soon challenged. Maybe the prohibition on 15-year-olds marrying is an obsolescent form of age discrimination. If these are closer to Dr. Carson's real concerns, then the burden is on us liberals to evaluate these possibilities.

From my angle, any Baltimorean who has lived among gays and lesbians knows that they are productive citizens, wonderful neighbors and devoted parents. In this light, any objection to their being married seems groundless. Perhaps this view is mistaken; if so, Dr. Carson's rejoinder deserves a hearing. After all, his is hardly a fringe view; tens of millions of Americans agree with him.

The extreme liberal backlash (a column in another local paper suggests that Dr. Carson's next surgery should be on his own brain) is another case of intellectual arrogance. It echoes the hubris of their malicious brethren on the conservative flanks. It sees the opponent as so brainwashed, biased by media and self-deluded that he or she is simply not capable of understanding or thinking through the issues.

Elected officials and media critics like to point out that the enemies of democracy reside in foreign lands, potential terrorists and fundamentalists who despise us. What is clear is that, as exemplified by the furor over Benjamin Carson, the real enemies of democracy also dwell in this country.

College, Inc.:
A Right-Winger's Dream

Is higher education a bastion of liberalism? Does it undermine its own principles of diversity by discriminating against certain political minorities?

Numerous conservatives contend that the answers to both questions are obvious. At least since Allan Bloom's *Closing of the American Mind* 25 years ago, critics have complained that colleges and universities are being overtaken and corrupted by liberalism - and even worse, "socialism." This victory has sparked not only a pernicious disregard for traditional education; it has also led to a degenerate climate where conservatives feel they are victimized as a minority. (As an example, a full-time college professor asserted on this page recently that he and other conservative academics feel they are targets of bias.)

Such complaints are ill-founded. During the last several decades, the academic world has increasingly become a conservative's dream: a citadel of capitalism. Yes, surveys show that most college professors claim some vague allegiance to liberalism, but this has minor significance. While they are allotted their trendy moments and causes - sustainability, multiculturalism, ecosensitivity and the rest, too numerous to mention - academics are largely subsumed by a pervasive, conservative corporate climate.

This begins with students. For years, they have been considered consumers and customers. They are investing in their future by taking out substantial loans to attend classes. Thus, schools expect to give them a "bang for their buck" or a "return for being a stakeholder." In precorporate academic life, orientation was a voluntary campus visit that lasted a couple of hours. Now it is often a mandatory two-day event to ensure that students are committed to their first major investment.

Faculty members contribute to this climate. Whereas in pre-corporate academic life a syllabus was one or two pages, today it serves as a quasi-legal document that runs up to 10 pages, replete with duties, deadlines and punishments. Students might be required to sign such documents, as if they are participating in a business contract. And it is their loss if they neglect to read the fine print.

The hierarchal and competitive nature of today's academic world should also please conservatives. Chancellors are now regarded as CEOs rather than as scholars hoping to nourish the college's intellectual traditions. Most readers know of the exorbitant money paid to college football and basketball coaches and how the millions of dollars pharmaceutical giants pour into research threaten scholarly integrity. Less known is that numerous professors are accorded superstar status. As free agents, they command huge salaries and reduced work loads (even jobs for their spouses) from schools courting their services. Institutions can afford these superstars since much of their profits rely on a large and inexpensive labor pool of adjunct professors and graduate teaching assistants. And the superstars, liberal or not, acquiesce to this capitalist structure.

Like Fortune 500 companies pushing their employees to increase revenues, colleges and universities continually expand. Higher enrollment, more land and extra campuses are continually sought. One local university wiped out acres of urban forest to build a soccer stadium. Another school razed historic buildings to put up more dorms or parking garages.

Objections from diversity enthusiasts were a footnote. Indeed, academic institutions resemble the little empires taught in political science and history courses.

The *Chronicle of Higher Education* recently devoted an entire issue to the making of the corporate university. A variety of observers describe how universities hire outside consultants to give them an identity, market their reputation, and devise catchy slogans for multimedia exposure. Gaye Tuchman, a sociologist from Connecticut, drew a parallel between the audit culture of big business and the accountability obsession on college campuses. She depicted the mundane routines in which administrators, staff members, teachers and students are repeatedly asked to answer surveys and questionnaires that ostensibly help them to endlessly assess one another.

Being a college teacher is, in my view, a privileged position. In light of this sketch of the academic world, it is unfathomable how conservatives and professors continue to lament—whine might be more accurate—the rise of socialism on campus. The self-righteous pieties of liberal academics are mostly ripples in a very large lake of corporate culture.

Moral Confusion at the End of Life

A kind and good-natured neighbor died last week. He always wanted to die in the peace and comforts of home, as his wife did 15 years ago. After a bad fall, an ambulance whisked him away. He wound up in a strange and sterile room, his body invaded by wires and tubes to the very end.

Will last year's health care overhaul - or any other proposal - be able to address this moral travesty? Public responses to this all-too-familiar experience are often sparked by those gifted in stoking the rhetorical flames of outrage and feigned compassion. "Death panel, "playing God" or "dying with dignity" are nice catchphrases, but they do little to clarify the obstacles before us.

A major problem is that we rely on several different moral guidelines. While helpful for everyday matters, they have short-comings when applied to life-and-death issues. For example, a version of the golden rule appears in nearly every major religion. Its secular variation appears in the seminal thought of Immanuel Kant, who believed we should never treat another rational being solely as a thing or object.

Yet the golden rule is not particularly adept in helping us prepare for suffering and dying. The axiom that "I treat others as I would want to be treated" obscures the fact that humans are quite distinct in their ways of dealing with mortal issues. I may be a wimp when it comes to pain and suffering, but for others pain inspires creativity, heroism or insight. To have them be treated as I would like to be treated is presumptuous on my part.

Contemporary health care is also a capitalist mega-industry. According to business writer Albert Carr, following the golden rule in a business climate is tantamount to inviting bankruptcy. Despite well-intentioned efforts to discuss candidly patients' preparation for dying, doctors and administrators work within the shadows of billion-dollar enterprises where deception and manipulation often prevail.

Some thinkers contend that a universal respect for individual human rights is a sensible alternative to the Golden Rule. Let rational individuals decide for themselves the circumstances in which they choose to live or die, then be sure to inform family and medical experts of these decisions.

Yet even this concept has drawbacks. It professionalizes death by requiring the oversight of lawyers as well as medical and psychological experts. Moreover, the wishes we announce when vibrant and healthy can alter when we start to deal with various stages of illness and disease. Numerous psychiatrists claim that a wish to die is not an expression of a rational mind but rather a symptom of depression. So the proper response may be treatment instead of granting the wish.

A third moral approach, social utility, is not anchored by the premise that all human lives have inherent and equal value. Guided by the "greatest happiness for the greatest number" principle, this approach looks to actions and laws that assess the benefits we receive from and the contributions we make to the overall good. Individual lives have relative worth. Today's most prominent advocate of social utility is Peter Singer. He has argued, for example, that a seeing-eye dog offers greater utility than a severely handicapped newborn, and hence is more deserving to live. This would also apply to the elderly who need extraordinary and expensive medical care.

This approach works when dealing with distant strangers, but it can be unwieldy when our friends or family members are involved. Mr. Singer himself was unable to follow social utility principles when his aging mother became very ill and he opted for extraordinary measures to sustain her. His critics were aghast. And his own response was somewhat flippant - that he, too, has trouble living up to his own ideals.

In any event, thinkers and moralists since Socrates and Seneca have encouraged humans to learn the art of dying: to prepare to live their last days on their own terms. Encumbered by medical advances, financial drives and litigious fears, the lessons of the sages remain more elusive than ever, as family members of my very kind neighbor sadly realized.

Burden of 'Buy the Book'

Need a last-minute book as a Christmas present for a thoughtful friend? Have a teenager who might be inspired by the imaginations and insights found in good writing? If so, you can forget about gift-wrapping a college textbook. Textbooks are unwieldy. They are often uninspiring, regardless of the initial enthusiasm that sparked their publication. And they are expensive - easily outpacing the lavish coffee-table productions featured in most bookstores.

Every year, the outcry over the rising cost of textbooks is heard anew. Though tuitions and faculty salaries are also increasing, more controversy is stirred over the cost of books that hold little appeal to the average reader. Worse, for the students required to buy them, a textbook often seems less a treasured memento of a sound education than a burden to unload once the final exam is over. Now Maryland officials are promising to address this problem.

Recently, university chancellors as well as faculty representatives have been issuing orders and conducting meetings aimed at alleviating the high costs of textbooks. Curiously, part of the problem, according to an assistant dean at Morgan State, is that most faculty are either unaware or indifferent to the prices of their required readings. Numerous proposals are bandied about, often hinging on more and better use of the Internet (as if students are not already more techno-savvy than administrators and faculty) and the voluntary vigilance of faculty (a recalcitrant lot). Neither option will do the trick.

Textbooks are a formidable industry. When all goes well, the consumers are satisfied and the text's producers gain steady and occasionally sizable profits. But a textbook is expensive to produce, taking considerable time and energy from a variety of specialists. Professors are paid for their comments on the prospectus or early draft. Copy editors are hired to scrutinize the material.

Designers are employed to enhance the format of the cover and chapters. And permissions run a high tab.

Used textbooks, another formidable industry, present a special problem. They offer college stores relief from the headache of finding storage for returns. Although the industry's practice of buying nearly any book seems commendable, the prices paid are ridiculously low. So effective is this market that if a new textbook does not make a profit within two years, it is virtually dead. Several fixes might be considered.

One is to drastically lower the original price, adding a small but fair transfer fee each time the textbook is resold. This fee could reimburse the authors and publishers. Second, instead of entire new editions, publishers could provide updated, inexpensive manuals. For example: The basic principles of introductory logic - deductive and inductive reasoning - have not changed much in the last century. Yet the logic text I use is in its ninth edition. To incorporate recent foibles of illogic committed by politicians, advertisers and commentators, a modest 30- to 40-page paperback would suffice. A third idea is to turn hefty and cumbersome textbooks into shorter, multivolume sets. This could allow professors flexibility in selecting one feature of a text without expecting students to buy the entire product. The introductory ethics anthology I published contained 88 selections. To fit them within 500 pages, the print was small and the margins crowded. To assign all the readings in a single semester would be impossible, if not cruel. Were the readings separated into three smaller volumes, faculty and students could have greater say in whether they wanted to focus on the historical thinkers, current dispute or literary figures with philosophical insights.

And the price would be lower.

In any event, publishers and professors should rethink the role of textbooks. With some effort and imagination, lucid and thoughtful textbooks could be available to audiences outside the classroom. They could even make good presents, some future Christmas.

Secularism requires a leap of faith, too

Learning that more than 6 million Jews perished in Nazi concentration camps, numerous survivors understandably became atheists. For many others, their religious beliefs were surprisingly strengthened. Are those who have been subjected to the cruelties of their fellow humans also victims of their own self-delusion and manipulation by clever priests? Yes, according to philosopher Crispin Sartwell.

In a Jan. 3 article sparked by reflections of a funeral for an acquaintance who committed suicide, Mr. Sartwell is dumbfounded over how otherwise rational persons still embrace religious convictions. History teaches us, and current events remind us, of the many horrors inflicted by those with contrary but impassioned convictions. Even alone, Mr. Sartwell observes, "systems of religious belief are ... arbitrary and obviously ridiculous."

Given how bizarre these systems are, Mr. Sartwell asks, "Why should you believe?" Since antiquity, thinkers of various stripes have counseled us to consider this question. Moreover, they also expect us to live according to our answers. Religious answers are often tempting. They offer a purpose in life, speak to ordinary hopes and fears, raise the prospects for justice and goodness and give a sense of the sacred. However, answers based on immeasurable, intangible and sometimes fantastic notions certainly make believers seem gullible.

Nietzsche, an inspiring thinker and vociferous critic of Judaism and Christianity, would share Mr. Sartwell's skepticism. But he cautioned against skepticism as an end in itself, for people need to believe. Indeed, what matters for most people is not that they muster the will to believe what is true, but simply that they have something—indeed, anything—in which to believe. In Nietzsche's sardonic words, most of us would rather believe in nothing than not to believe at all.

Does secular society offer an adequate alternative, as Mr. Sartwell suggests? Its record is not particularly enlightening. We can chuckle smugly over stories about sacrificing virgins and resurrecting messiahs, but the story of secular societies is equally numbing. Many thrived only on the wave of slavery, colonialism and jingoism. The bloodbaths that highlight recent memory have little to do with the monotheism skeptics find incredulous. Ten million or so in Stalin's Soviet Union, 2 million plus in Pol Pot's Cambodia, millions more in Mao's China.

Secular society today entices us with high-priced politics, global economies, scientific research and communication technologies. Still, these are not entirely rational enterprises. Rather than replacing irrational religions, they have ushered in new gods. They too demand our faith—faith in the legitimacy of presidential elections, the blessings of NAFTA, the miracles of medicine and the lords of Microsoft.

How many of us, though, can really offer an informed and rational case for this faith, other than it promises you or me good things? Is the promise, for example, of more choices for a consumer at eBay or the mall more compelling than the promise of paradise or justice for all?

An outsider who surveys our prison, transportation, marketing and public education systems could easily conclude that they are, in Mr. Sartwell's eloquent terms, "just a wee bit cracked." These irrational systems nevertheless draw millions of believers. And when pushed or challenged, their staunchest supporters easily proffer justifications for sacrificing the well-being of many other lives. Secularism, in other words, could just as well be another religion, but on the pretense that it is not.

So, backatcha, Mr. Sartwell. Perhaps the recent and fiery explosions arising from the great monotheistic religions are only surface tremors lingering from the convictions of our ancestors. To explain this mess as efforts in knitting together the erratic threads of the world hardly suffices.

More likely, the real gods are the ones still disguising themselves. More power to you if you believe in them. But why should you?

Shooting down law and order

For those seeking the newest role models, a Baltimore County grand jury has offered two candidates: Matthew and Tony Geckle, owners of a cement factory in Owings Mills. Despite admitting to shooting three unarmed intruders, killing one, they were indicted for neither first nor second-degree murder. Not even manslaughter. No doubt this episode contains a human drama: Elements of fear, possibilities of loss, two devoted brothers enduring a personal crisis. Moreover, the vigilante–a label the Geckles accept–is a mainstay of American history.

Those supporting the grand jury's verdict could contend that a concrete factory is as essential to our survival (what is modern life without highways, stadiums and shopping malls) as livestock, crops or clothing were in earlier times for ranchers, farmers or seamstresses. They also were granted the right to protect their livelihood by any means necessary. The grand jury, however, has extended the notion of self- protection to include businessmen holing up in their offices with shotguns, waiting in the dark night to shoot unarmed intruders in the back.

This decision sends a message more powerful than any violent Hollywood movie, rap song, or athletic scandal. It declares that the legacy of vigilantes–from lynch mobs hanging their victims on a tree to Bernard Goetz shooting suspected thugs in a New York subway–casts new light on our models of justice. It tells citizens that whenever they feel threatened by another, they may stretch the boundaries of the law by taking it into their own hands. Presumably, then, any of us can now act as the proverbial "judge, jury and executioner."

There is something strange and frightening in the grand jury's decision. When police, for example, shoot an alleged lawbreaker, charges of brutality and sporadic riots erupt. Yet police have much more training about when and when not to fire on a suspect. If even they undergo lapses in judgment, imagine how easily ordinary people can mistakenly shoot someone suspected of bringing them harm—a high school bully, a scorned lover, a corporate tycoon or a computer hacker.

Strange, too, that Tony Geckle has been eerily silent. Perhaps his own reflections of the event are now tormenting him. As soldiers and police officers painfully confess, to kill another human being can be a haunting experience.

By all published accounts Mr. Geckle is a decent person. In similar circumstances, would you or I not keep replaying the moment: Did I panic? Was it too dark to discern the situation? In 1902, Owen Wister published "The Virginian." One of the first cowboy novels, it relates a scene with posses, rustlers and vigilantes: `Judge Henry,' said Molly Wood, `have you come to tell me that you think well of lynching?' He met her. `Of burning Southern Negroes in public, no. Of hanging Wyoming cattle-thieves in private, yes. You perceive there's a difference, don't you?' `Not in principle," answered the girl."

To the contrary, insists the Baltimore County grand jury. Gather up some bravado, tune up the arsenal and, in the name of self- protection, shoot first and ask questions later. And if by chance you or I cannot tell the difference, as long as we cite the absence of police, complain we have had enough, then we, too, should expect to escape charges of murder. Even manslaughter.

To choose to die on one's own terms

"This is is the only way I want to die: To make my death the occasion of a crime is an idea that causes my head to spin."

Is this a quote found by investigators of the Sharon Lopatka crime? Could this be one of the unerased messages expressing her secret desires on the Internet?

The death of the Marylander has drawn widespread attention. For months she had been planning her death by trying to find someone to assist her in a spectacular and, in most of our eyes, horrible experience. So far, commentators have largely worried whether Sharon Lopatka's death will affect the use of telecommunications by the crazies of the world. Yet the epigraph above was made long before cyberspace. It was written in a jail some 200 years ago by the Marquis de Sade. He was hardly the first to link his own death with crime. There is a long and even noble history to this idea.

While everyone knows that Socrates was made to drink hemlock, most of us forget how Socrates consulted his friends in order to help decide how he should make his own death. Should Socrates shamefully escape prison and live unjustly, or drink the hemlock and let his dying be testimony to the law's committing a greater crime by executing him? That he chose to die earlier and on his own terms rather than desperately cling to an unworthy life did not draw the moral rebuke of his friends. In their eyes, according to the Phaedo story in which Socrates dies, he was the "wisest, justest and best" of all men.

We might be reminded how Christianity grew during its infancy. Persuasion of potential converts was more drastic than manipulating target groups who subscribe to cable TV. The early saints often enticed possible Christians by making their own deaths a crime. The chronicles of Christian martyrs testify to excruciating efforts in making one's own death a criminal matter.

"Yields to God alone" "How beautiful is the spectacle to God when a Christian does battle with pain," wrote the early Christian historian Minucius Felix, for the dying saint "raises his liberty against kings and princes, and yields to God alone." If beautiful for God, imagine the effect on mere mortals witnessing the event. Which of us non-believers could resist the call to belief upon such a sight?

Sharon Lopatka's death obviously does not carry the stature of the above examples. To simplify her demise, however, to a discussion about anonymous chat rooms or kinky sex only reveals our own obsessions more clearly. This simplification has the added effect of keeping us in the fog about how her death reflects a recurring human concern—making death one's own. Nietzsche once speculated, "Many die too late and some too early. Still the doctrine sounds strange: Die at the right time."

As far as we outsiders can tell, Sharon Lopatka made a strange decision about this doctrine. Perhaps only her family and friends have a sense of the inner torment, confusion or fascination that drove her to North Carolina. Maybe her spectacular departure will be memorialized as a cultural or legal event. Could a Lopatka bill await the next Congress' deliberations over policing the information highway?

Whatever our speculations, we should be wary of feigning moral indignation or righteousness over Sharon Lopatka. She is an extension of a culture unable to convict Jack Kevorkian of a crime where, unlike more celebrated death crimes, the suspect freely admits his complicity. This inability is a sign of moral paralysis. Talking about Sharon Lopatka's tragic death only in terms of computers or perversion can only sustain this paralysis.

5
Sundry Favorites

Introduction

Some of these could have been placed in earlier chapters. They are here for disjointed reasons, mostly personal. Two or three sprung from times I watched a popular TV program with my daughter and son, or when I tortured them with Beatles music when driving them around. Actually, they wound up enjoying my beloved group, particularly the movie "Yellow Submarine." A couple of the selections were 700 word take-offs from more academic projects. When rereading the essays now, I'm grateful the editors let me get away with some things. I wish more people would appreciate how Baltimore's op-ed editors encourage a range of perspectives.

The Essays

We never forget the first time. It could be the first time falling in love, going through great joy or disappointment, having someone close die, driving a car, moving out. "Gd=Comic" was my first op-ed essay. At the time Maryland began offering vanity license plates where people could pay extra to have their own selected letters and numbers. Most would opt for nicknames or personal tastes. "Ck-Mate" likely meant the driver plays chess, or "Dogs 4 Evr" indicates the driver dotes on canines. Given human nature, inevitably there were requests for political views, obscenities, and mysterious omens which the Motor Vehicles Department had to scrutinize. What surprised me then was getting paid for the essay. If you break down the hours to compose an essay on an hourly scale, it's less than minimum wage. (Many papers no longer pay for guest columns.) Still, a 7,000 word academic article gets me a line on my CV, while 700 words for a newspaper meant I could treat a buddy to snacks and drinks.

One of my weaknesses is lists. I read them with trepidation and suspicion—who are these people believing they are so knowledgeable to identify the 100 greatest movies, baseball players or rock n' roll hits? When I disagree with them, I scoff at the idiocy of the voting committee. But when they feature my top choices, I abruptly praise the selectors for their acuity and insight. There have been disparate lists that claim Babe Ruth or Willie Mays is the greatest baseball player of all-time, "Citizen Kane" or "The Godfather" as top movie in history, "The Simpsons" or "Seinfeld" as best ever television program.

In ranking the greatest rock and roll albums of all time, poll after poll agrees on one—"Sergeant Pepper's Lonely Hearts Club Band." Purists belittle the album as too high tech, a departure from the roots of rock or the work of self-indulgent superstars. Regardless, this Beatles album was both a culmination and departure point for modern music, not to mention a cultural event.

The essay on casinos offers a lesson on being turned down. Op-ed editors have numerous tasks and receive innumerable submissions each day. So most rejections are polite and general "Thanks, but we'll pass on this one." Sometimes they will offer a brief comment, such as "Nice essay, but not very newsworthy for now," or "we've already run some commentaries on this topic." I knew the issue on legalizing casinos in Maryland had received considerable attention from *The Baltimore Sun*, particularly from politicians and researchers on the economic benefits and social effects of state sanctioned casinos. I hoped my angle on how a mathematician explained the complete deception of computer-driven slots would be a distinctive angle. Facing the variety of news events and controversies every day, an op-ed editor has to draw the line on how much coverage on a specific topic becomes too much.

Several drafts of these essays have been presented to my students for review. Once they overcome the hesitancy in commenting on a professor's writing, their suggestions are quite helpful. Undergrads might not know the technical terms for a grammatical or rhetorical miscue, but they have been surprisingly helpful when recognizing an awkward phrase or unclear passage. The enduring controversy over where or how to draw the line began with my contribution to a book on logical fallacies. During one logic course, I asked students to review an abridged version for a possible op-ed piece audience. If the essay gets accepted, their reward is no class the following Friday.

"In the Right Direction" is one of my favorites because the editor lets me get away with a Nietzsche epigraph: "In reality, there has been only one Christian—and he died on the cross." Many of my essays (and more academic works) begin with an epigraph, usually retained but sometimes deleted by the editor. An epigraph is a pithy quote that can introduce a tone, insight, or wry point to the subsequent writing.

Maybe this is a pathological habit on my part, but I often rely on epigraphs to be guideposts. It might also be my silent homage to the master of epigraphs—Nietzsche. This essay addresses an ongoing controversy about prayer in schools, and whether Biblical passages convey any useful perspective on a country that composes five percent of the world's population but uses forty percent of its energy.

Writing about character education stems from a larger project on who learns or teaches the virtues and vices. This controversy goes back to Socrates when he continually asked why it is quite evident that there is vice but no one claims to teach the vices. To the contrary, most people and institutions insist that they teach only the virtues and develop moral character.

My interest here was on the on-going debate over whether school teachers should be required to teach moral character. Elementary school teachers have 20-30 children each day; high school teachers will have five different classes with 20-30 students in each class. I'm not convinced that these teachers, in addition to their specialized subjects, should also be focused on the moral character of so many children, particularly if the rest of society tempts and entertains children with so many vices. It seems an impossible expectation.

The Baltimore Chronicle was originally *The City Dweller.* It was considered an alternative newspaper—long before the current hoopla about alternative news. For almost a year I worked for the *Dweller,* obtaining advertisements from local businesses, interviewing individuals devoted to Baltimore City, and writing four or five news and feature articles for every issue.

Our office was in a dank basement on Maryland Avenue. Above was a brothel. The editor-in-chief then was Larry Krause, founder of the paper. Several times Larry and I were working late on weekends to meet the deadline for getting all material to the printer's while upstairs was quite excited with patrons enjoying their payday. Eventually the *City Dweller* became *the Baltimore Chronicle* with a new editor-in-chief, Alice Cherbonnier. This has little to do with the topic science and religion as discussed here, but thought you might enjoy the historical backdrop.

The only reason I pursued the story about a Goucher professor suddenly dismissed was due to my relation to the college through conferences, colleagues and teaching a couple of courses. From what I read or heard, the case seemed very flimsy. It involved someone from Rwanda with alleged links to an administration that imprisoned, tortured and randomly executed citizens suspected of disloyalty. Maybe the teacher was guilty, though the last time I checked there was still legal uncertainty. What struck me here is that Goucher's president wrote a letter to the Sun in response to my piece, and it was replete with vague and obligatory comments about following protocol.

This essay was published before the subsequent massacres on college campuses. In this light, my approach was clearly shortsighted and I now realize that Goucher College must have faced a very difficult dilemma. In rereading these essays, there are several that I'd like to have revised not because of the writing but because of an uneven focus. This is one of them.

Is it hyperbole to propose that the modern image of evil is a terrorist? Unlike the image of twentieth century models of evil—say Hitler or Stalin—today's image keeps changing. The face of the terrorists always seems to surprise. Some are, in commentator Ann Coulter's words, swarthy Muslim men from the Middle East. Her myopic angle ignores the faces that also include teenage suicide bombers, alienated young men from small towns, crazed Americans who gun down worshipers in rural churches, among so many others.

Some of the points in this essay reflected a more academic paper on terrorism and torture that I was developing. But the central theme was stirred by seeing the many faces of terrorism on the hit TV series, "24." For several years my daughter, son and I were devoted fans. So the academic approach on terrorism and the popular dramas via television made for a fortuitous combination.

Not particularly religious, I remain an unabashed idolater. I do not belong to any denomination that worships a specific god, but I have a pantheon of humans whose accomplishments I greatly admire. The Beatles have been life-long members of this pantheon. There are Beatle bashers and malcontents who insist they are an overrated band and a collection of so-so abilities. Perhaps.

Yet Marc Lewisohn contends the Beatles are historical figures, as he just published via a major press an 800 page first volume of his trilogy on their lives and work. A radio station in Philadelphia (WXPN) has a daily 10:30 morning feature that plays four songs by the Beatles, covers of their music, or songs by the individuals after the break-up. Once a year a Baltimore radio station (WTMD) devotes an entire day to playing the Beatles catalogue on vinyl; it is their biggest fundraiser day. Whenever a poll on the greatest rock albums of all time gets updated, the Beatles continue to place five of the top fifteen, *Rubber Soul, Revolver, Sgt. Peppers, The White Album,* and *Abbey Road.* They broke up in 1970. Current artists regularly cite being influenced by their legacy and people of all ages continue listening to them. No other modern musical artist comes close to receiving such attention.

In this light, it seems fair to say that the Beatles are to rock and popular music as Bach and Beethoven are to classical—still the sound of the future.

Gd=Comic

With the constitutional furor over license plates at a momentary standstill, a review of the lessons might be useful.

On the practical side, there could be minor benefits in having "God Is" on license plates. It certainly is easy to remember. And five letters make for less cleaning. But let's not neglect possible disadvantages. A scurrilous atheist might sabotage the auto. An envious Christian could want the plates for his trophy room.

Aside from that, I have trouble seeing what the fuss is about. Advocates believe the license tags allow forms of free expression, and if subtle forms of obscenity are permitted, then so should overt claims of piety. Atheists and sundry constitutionalists remind us that the founding fathers wanted to prohibit the state from association with or tacit approval of a particular religious belief.

Overlooked in this debate is the expression itself. "God Is" does not say a whole lot. While it could tell us something about those who pay $25 to advertise God next to an exhaust pipe or those who sit in traffic jams and can't find something better to worry about, the phrase itself tells nothing about divinity. Philosophers have a fancy rebuttal to this type of expression: "Existence is not a predicate." When we talk about God and His qualities, that God exists is neither assured nor demonstrated.

This prevents, for example, the kind of exchange in which a theist states, "God is all knowing," When the atheist responds, "God is not all knowing," the theist victoriously declares, "Aha! So you do believe in God, because by doubting His omniscience you acknowledge His existence. Library shelves are filled with volumes on this topic.

Spare yourself the headache of reading them and simply turn to everyday language. When a baby arrives parents don't say, "Little Joe is." They say "Joe is born." And when Joe is getting up in years, friends don't ask "Is Joe?" Instead, they discreetly inquire, "Is Joe healthy?" And when Joe finally departs, do you have see obituaries and mourners announce, "Joe is not?" Of course not. "Joe is dead" makes the point.

On the other hand, there is the view that God cannot have a predicate. A name, any name, tends to define or limit. That is why we attach labels to things, so when we want an apple we don't get a fig or a pear. If God is infinite or boundless, any label ascribed to God by human artifice introduces the following paradox: If we believe in the infinitude of God, then we can't say it. But once we say it, can we still believe it?

Here rationalism and mysticism confront each other. From this angle "God Is" comes as close as any utterance in expressing divine intuition. Whether mystical truths can be captured on vanity license plates is another matter.

Most people probably recognize the ambiguity of "God Is," hence their good sense in attending to more mundane concerns. Fundamentalists of a Christian or constitutional bent, shameless in their self-righteousness, dislike ambiguity. It leads to messy confusions. That they appeal to a master of messy confusions, Maryland's Department of Motor Vehicles, for settling this dispute is amusing.

It is hard to imagine that such an irony could be perpetrated by mere mortals. Perhaps that could even answer part of the theological quandary: God is…a comedian. In abbreviated form: "Gd=Comic." Now let's see what happens if someone squeezes that onto a license plate.

Sgt. Pepper's turns 50; At the half century mark, it's still the 'greatest album of all time'

When the mode of music changes, the walls of the city shake. —Plato

Today marks the 50th anniversary of the release of The Beatles' masterpiece, "Sgt. Pepper's Lonely Hearts Club Band." In polls taken by rock and roll critics, including the latest ranking in Rolling Stone magazine, Sgt. Pepper's is invariably picked as the greatest album of all time.

According to rock journalist Langdon Winner, who happened to be traveling through big cities and small towns in early June of 1967, every radio station and cafeteria juke box was constantly featuring this latest Beatles album. Stereos in Europe and America played it endlessly. Young people partied to it all night and quickly learned the lyrics to sing along. In Mr. Winner's words, "The closest Western Civilization has come to unity since the Congress of Vienna in 1815 was the week Sgt. Pepper was released."

Has any music or work of art been lauded in such terms since then? This is not just another pitiful attempt at Baby Boomer nostalgia. Many current musicians - including Kanye West, Tori Amos and the Flaming Lips - still point to Sgt. Pepper's as revolutionizing the options for creating music in a studio that cannot be performed live on stage.

Sgt. Pepper's appeared as a spectacle rather than just a collection of songs. The album was the first to print all the lyrics of the songs on the back cover. The front cover was unique and expensive, featuring an array of the Beatles idols, mostly Americans, including W. C. Fields, Dion, Dylan, Brando, Shirley Temple, Marilyn Monroe, Laurel &Hardy, Edgar Allan Poe and Mae West. Other figures, such as Gandhi, Oscar Wilde or Lewis Carroll, had enduring influences on the Beatles' social and artistic developments.

Then there is the music. Each song surprises with new sounds and stories. No longer are The Beatles singing about she loves you, he has no reply, or she has just given you a ticket to ride. A mere three years after wanting to hold someone's hand, they were focused on friendships, carnivals, meter maids, teenagers leaving home, a son's drawing that he calls "Lucy in the Sky," news items about deadly car accidents, troubles at school. Three guitars and a drum no longer suffice; Sgt. Pepper's is the first rock album to incorporate a British orchestra, Hindu chants as well as tuneful sentiments from the big band era.

There was considerable debate about how best to experience this spectacle. Some fans preferred headphones and the solitary intensity. Others insisted on the communal moment, replaying the album at a party throughout the night. Johnny Rivers referred to it in the 1973 Billboard top 20 song "Summer Rain," when he celebrates how everyone "kept on playing Sgt. Pepper's Lonely Hearts Club Band."

Sgt. Pepper's admittedly has its detractors. For many critics, including devoted Beatle fans, it is self-indulgent. The Beatles now seem to present themselves as elite artists while abandoning their stature as the preeminent rock and roll band. And given their fame, this album spawned imitators ushering out all sorts of loopy and annoying psychedelic concept albums. More disappointing for others was that The Beatles were known for their candor, humor and earthiness; but Sgt. Pepper's seems less authentic, too enamored with glitzy studio techniques.

Some music and art gets discussed so much that it is difficult to experience it anew. Sgt. Pepper's falls victim to this. Still, you should try to disregard the hoopla and listen to it with fresh ears, as if the first time. When you reach the closing sequence of three songs, you begin to realize the album's power. You hear two thumping rock songs that lead into the apocalyptic "A Day in The Life." The lyrics are about everyday desperation, absurdity, insight, good cheer and joy. No wonder it made people say they were glad to be alive.

Sgt. Pepper's changed the mode of music. It still shakes the walls of modern sounds. It is to rock music what Beethoven's Ninth was to symphonic music - a masterpiece that was both a culmination and a departure point. It truly is the greatest rock album ever.

Casinos and Today's Scam Artists

For Jeff and Patty

*"Even as I approach the gambling hall, as soon as
I hear, two rooms away, the jingle of money poured
onto the table, I almost go into convulsions."* —
Dosteyvsky, The Gambler

For the longest time these sorts of convulsions prompted human beings to talk about vice and social corruption. Today they are translated into easy and enormous bucks not only for big business, but big government as well. The emerging rematch between former Governor Robert Ehrlich and current Governor Martin O'Malley and their views on slots betrays an uncanny similarity.

It is now undeniable that both candidates agree and condone that the State of Maryland should assume the role of scam artists. The easy prey will be their own citizens and neighbors. There is no other way to understand their mutual embrace of legalized slot machines.

Consider the slot machine itself. Its pre-1980s forerunner, found in sundry locales as bowling alleys and cafeterias, was aptly named the "one armed bandit." Operated by gears, pulleys and cylinders, it usually featured various fruits, blanks and wild cards. If a machine had three wheels, with each wheel featuring fifteen or twenty icons, players felt that they could learn and eventually beat the machine, maybe hit the jackpot. It was assumed that a machine gradually developed a bias. As its mechanical parts started getting worn, patterns or tendencies supposedly became more pronounced. Learning this and finding the exact time to pull its "arm" could slightly tilt the advantage to the bettor, and defeating the wanna-be-bandit.

Thus gamblers felt they could eventually make reliable predictions and control the game. Obviously, this requires lots of time, concentration, and money spent on losing before detecting the game's inner weaknesses. One could first wind up broke.

Today's slot machines offer no such challenge. They are run by elaborate computers. Continually scrambling the possible combinations across five windows, they make it impossible for even an alert gambling mind to keep track of any pattern or bias. The "arm" is strictly a gimmick. As mathematician Joseph Mazur lucidly describes in his remarkable study of numbers, odds and the gambler's illusion, once a coin or token is dropped into the slot machine, the outcome is already determined. Those seconds of rolling images and pulling the "arm" are tricks. They have no bearing on the final display. Promotional signs about the casino paying off 95%, the clamoring of bells to announce an occasional winner, and free drinks to any player all contribute to the illusion.

In this sense slot machines, and anyone benefiting from them, are pulling off a scam. A fair gamble means that each participant has a chance at winning. A scam means one participant is being duped into believing he or she has a chance of winning in the long run, but in fact does not. The incessant marketing of the rare jackpot winner underscores the scam.

Scams succeed because the mark is weak or ignorant. Indeed, there is considerable speculation that not all gambling is about winning. To the contrary, some experts claim that gamblers are psychological masochists who want to lose. Others hypothesize that they seek something akin to a high. For example, one friend still remembers a heart thumping moment when he was on a roll at the craps table and dozens of people were betting on or against him.

Another theory holds that adult gamblers are still reworking the trauma of being potty-trained. For them money symbolizes bodily waste. As a baby or toddler, the future slots player was suddenly forbidden to delight in the body's various pleasures; hence the phrases about "shooting one's wad" or "filthy money." Next time you visit a casino, observe how frequently players are fondling their coins and bills. For them, the issue is not leaving ahead but simply the duration spent at the machine or table. These explanations, however, bring us to the shadows of pathology.

In any event, Mr. Ehrlich and Mr. O"Malley agree that the State of Maryland should engage in this con game, taking advantage of citizens with potential convulsions rather than protect them. To that extent, we should debate if either is fit to be our next governor.

Who gets to draw the line and why?

Quick quiz: What do these disparate news items have in common? A comedian displays on social media an effigy of a decapitated head of an American president. Maryland legislators debate the legal ramifications of allowing topless women on public beaches. A movie features a character with autism and is publicly denounced by a mother with an autistic child.

Figure it out? These items share the human complexities about drawing the line. In each case there were concerns about crossing or violating it. This issue is not limited to news reports. It permeates all phases of our lives. The frustrated parent admonishes the kids that this is the last straw in messing up their rooms. Angry neighbors point to the local partiers and assert their disruptive revelry has gone too far. Playground adversaries place a long stick between them and dare one another to step over it.

In many areas of our lives we address this problem by establishing and enforcing laws and rules. How fast is too fast on the roadway is defined by speed limits. Judges decide on the proper amount of punishment for convicted criminals. In sports, you know you've crossed the line when you are out of bounds, reached the end zone, or wave your arms while passing the finish line. In these areas we know we have crossed the line because it has been authorized, declared and made visible.

In many areas of life, though, the line that might be crossed is not so obvious. Consider the initial examples. A comedian's success is often based on being daring and irreverent, even if appealing to our tastes for macabre humor. Decapitated heads have been displayed and mocked in the Bible, medieval Europe and contemporary terrorism. Yet where exactly is the line crossed that a comedian blundered in depicting a president this way? Only after an uproar reveals the invisible line does the apology appear.

As Maryland legislators now realize, drawing the line over public displays of human body parts is a nuanced controversy. On the beach there are aging men with fleshier breasts than many young women. Should not the floppy appendages of these geezers also be concealed while they meander along the boardwalk? The Greeks invented the notion of gymnasium; its etymology refers to naked bodies/exercise. For them the athletic body was most fit for intellectual and spiritual pursuits.

Maybe legislators should require that only sluggards and slothful types should adorn bathing suits in order to conceal their unfitness. Where do we draw the line about which naked human body respects family values and which one violates such values? And why?

There are many areas of human life where rules and laws about drawing the line are inept or unenforceable. So we rely on common sense or practical judgment. Common sense, however, is not that common, and practical judgment tends to succumb to our excessive desires and passions, our pride or myopic ambition.

We rarely know in advance where is the line that we later will regret we crossed. Yet many of our heroes and idols dare to test the extremes - one reason we admire them. And some of our most memorable experiences and stories are of moments when we, too, dared going too far.

There are also sad cases of those who shrink from this dare. Consider acquaintances, colleagues or friends who are going through a tough time, burdensome job or loveless marriage. We ask them - and ourselves - at what point do we draw the line and admit that we have to cross it? This cannot go on, we try to

convince one another. We begrudgingly fool ourselves by ins.
we somehow cannot recognize when enough is enough and t.
straw is broken.

The news highlights unfunny comedians and frustrated legislators, as they are fodder for our daily amusement. Yet their foibles
and transgressions echo our own. Most of us are unsure when to
cross the line that is invisible.

In the right direction

"In reality there has been only one Christian—and he died on the cross." —Nietzsche

To satisfy the combatants in the latest prayer-in-schools contest, I offer an easy solution. Give students a chance with prayer. More, let them try parts of the Bible throughout the day. Instead of worrying about whether a moment of silence to start the day will turn an MTV generation into a band of religious zealots, we should let them regularly cite sacred texts for each class.

Here is a sketch of the average day under my proposal:

Energized by homeroom's famed silent moment, eager students trot off to economics class. Here they might encounter the theory supporting additional tax relief or capital gains breaks for the wealthy. The yacht, learns our typical student, is a business investment, not a leisure vehicle. For this class it would be fitting to chant Jesus' classic on the ticket to heaven: "It is easier for a camel to go through the eye of a needle than for a rich man to enter the kingdom of heaven" (Matthew 19:24).

Next is history class. Here a 12-year-old might read of a time when 12-year-olds were considered property, subject to arranged marriages or forced labor. It was during such a time when children were rebuked from seeing Jesus. So let history begin with students together reading Jesus' response. "Let the children come to me, do not hinder them; for to such belongs the kingdom of God" (Mark 10: 13-14). Who knows, this might spark history students to pursue a cross-generational semester project about, say, how the right to own guns, public orphanages or dangerous schools are current ways of rebuking a child's sense of belonging.

Undaunted by the scary comparison, the average student heads for English class. First the teacher returns last week's essays full of red marks. Then the class recites Jesus' famous line: "Judge not and you will not be judged; condemn not, and you will not be condemned" (Luke 6:37).

Lunchtime. Students say grace, of course, but silently.

After recess students trudge on to social studies. Before turning to the pages on homelessness and deviance, they chant in unison Jesus' words: "Your sins are forgiven . . . I tell you, her sins, which are many, are forgiven for she loved much; but he who is forgiven little, loves little" (Luke 7: 47-48). This is a startling comment. Jesus does not explain immoral actions in terms of bad genes, personal malice or innate evil. Before students can finish thinking about this, though, the bell rings.

Finally, math class. A dumbfounded school official might wonder how a biblical passage can start a math class. I suggest a drill be a group meditation on a puzzle of how to feed 5,000 people on five loaves of bread and two fish. Everyone gets a crumb, muses a young idealist. Too impractical, speculates a hardened realist—better to feed the healthiest and ensure the survival of the species. A violation of rights, ponders the constitutional purist: whoever owns the food eats the food, so the starving do not have a right to another's property. This drill is to explain Jesus' solution when he said of the 5,000, "Bring them to me" (Matthew 14:18), and he fed all the people. (Hint: Jesus did not say anything about punishing welfare recipients.)

My proposal should satisfy the major sides of this dispute. Conservatives get more than what they are demanding, though often that is not enough. Constitutional purists and liberals should be content realizing that all the prayers in school will not corrupt the purity of American politics and culture—our devotion and sacrifices to television and computers are unshakable.

And multiculturalists should see this as a victory. After living in a country where immigrant children are unwanted, where politicians portray welfare mothers as happy in their poverty and fear-ridden neighborhoods, where 50 percent of the world's energy is used by 5 percent of its population, our students would reasonably conclude that the biblical passages they recite with each class are merely samples of a strange voice speaking of a strange culture.

It is a voice whose name is shared by billions. But as Nietzsche might put it, the voice is quite solitary. For it evokes a way of life with different hopes, different compassions and different spirits.

Character Education Cannot be Schooled

Play is like education of the body, character or mind ... The further removed play is from reality, the greater its educational value. For it does not teach facts, but rather develops aptitudes.—Roger Caillois

Baltimore City officials are poor-mouthing again over the issue of play areas for children. When the weather becomes hot, they try to close or cut the hours of swimming pools. With colder and shorter days approaching, they threaten to shut down numerous neighborhood recreation centers.

How strange that these officials can easily find the resources and tax breaks to support "play areas" for wealthy adults. When the Ravens or Orioles are at home, the city makes sure the police get their overtime pay to monitor the fans and traffic. To procure professional race car drivers for a Grand Prix play date, Baltimore officials are suddenly ingenious in obtaining monies for development, promotion and rebuilding downtrodden roads.

Where else is this oddity found besides Baltimore? Well, lots of places. Urban life, for the last three decades or longer, has seen a steady erosion of fertile space for children to play. This fact should not be attributed to lack of funds. It reflects a deliberate degradation by adults of the importance of play in a child's life.

Play is essential for children. It marks their first taste of freedom - and it is fun. They reach an important step in autonomy by leaving home voluntarily, negotiating directions and constraints with friends and strangers, and addressing their own mistakes. Play also introduces unexpected suspense and danger. It thus pushes children to learn about awkward spots, true friends and unruly adversaries - as well as the tensions within their own desires, interests and loyalties.

Most importantly, children at play are generally free from adults. Without the rules, evaluations and immediate supervision of parents, teachers and other authorities, children learn to deal with one another. They learn to coordinate, compromise or compete by their own imagination and wits.

A city's mayor and officials, and the adults who voted them into office, support or condone the degradation of play in urban life by the ritualistic threat to shut down pools or youth centers. If commuters demand easier access, then cities build more roads, garages and rails - deadly barriers for a child's independent mobility. The city goes out of its way to accommodate wealthy patrons who want special attention for their adult fun. But when neighborhood organizers offer their services to sustain local youth centers, as the case in the recent controversies over DeWees and Hampden, their efforts are upended with bureaucratic details.

Children have instead been offered two main alternatives. One, parents register them for continuous little leagues, clinics and tournaments in one or more sports. This can be expensive and is still largely supervised by adults. Two, parents and corporations entice them with video games so they can sit before their electronic shadows and twiddle their thumbs all afternoon. Upon mastering a game, they head for the nearest Game Stop to buy their next challenge, only to return to the sedentary indoors.

Compared to light rail lines, stadiums and Inner Harbor spectacles, swimming pools, well-kept parks and indoor youth centers are relatively inexpensive public places. They provide space for children to develop their own games while anticipating risky adventures and make-believe dramas. French sociologist Ro⸱ Caillois contends that play encourages children to briefly shape their own reality as a break from the reality imposed by parents and schools. This break should neither be devalued as frivolous nor demeaned, according to an old adage, as "a tool in the devil's workshop." It is a distinct reality that constitutes an essential part of a child's education.

Urban officials are unlikely to curtail their support for play dates among the wealthy. Earmarking a percentage of the profits for public education has been an ongoing promise and marketing ploy. But if they and voters are serious about the well-being of their children, they can support earmarking a percentage of profits not only for schools, but for the other half of a child's education - play.

Truth Science and Religion Have In Common

Religion and science do agree on at least one point: race does not exist. They both hold that there are white, black, red, or yellow races among human beings. The categories of Mongoloid Negroid or Caucasian are closer to fantasies than designators of real human beings. Indeed, according to their basic tenets, grouping humans by races makes about as much sense as grouping them according to their astrological signs.

The truth of this can be found in our origins. Strangely, at least two quite different origins have been spotted. One appears in sacred texts, the other in ancient bones and relics.

Genesis, the first book of the Bible, illustrates a religious perspective. It reports that humans will split up as nations and communities, but not as races. This was embraced by numerous splinter groups. For example, the Moravians, who in the 1700's settled around Winston-Salem, North Carolina, were aghast at how slavery was so central to American life. Their abhorrence of slavery was attributed less by a belief in human rights than by its falseness according to Biblical authority. Scriptures, despite what they sometimes depict about human cruelties, nevertheless make no mention of human races.

Modern science derives the truth about race from different origins—from the bones and artifacts of our ancient ancestors. Science relies on the credibility of empirical investigations and demonstrations. Hypotheses and educated guesses need evidence and thoughtful explanation. When paleontologists keep finding ever-older remnants of humanoids, they show us that humans have too much of a mix of similarities and differences to be understood in terms skin color and facial features. Most researchers conclude that the very notion of four or five human biological types is too simplistic and misleading to be scientific useful. The myth of race, anthropologist Ashley Montagu and his colleagues called it.

Obviously these accounts have contrasting stories and explanations. But the universal reach of their common truth is remarkable. Every religion seems to embrace some variation of the golden rule. We should love our neighbor regardless. Although exactly who is our neighbor can be a contentious issue, sacred tales speak of the disputes in terms other than race.

Empirical sciences do not appeal to divine authorities. Instead, they appeal to the authority of empirical evidence and analytic thought. To understand how the earliest human societies began, flourished or disappeared, the appeal to race contributes nothing. Scrutinizing the physical remains of our forebears—their skulls and DNA samples, their art work and utensils—scientists do not detect Latino, Native American or African. They, like religion, discover human groups, communities, nations, collectives, cults, sects, orders or families, but no races.

This commonality has been obscured by the intelligent design/evolution trial in Dover, Pennsylvania. The disputants about school curriculum highlight only the shortcomings of their adversary. The charges and counter charges become predictable: Religion does not appeal to independent criteria. Science cannot account for the miracle of the eye or heart. Religion overlooks the obvious lessons of nature. Science fails to persuade of any higher purpose to human life.

Those who seek some reconciliation by noting the examples of scientists who believe in a divinity or religious scholars who find evolution compatible with theism avoid the main controversies.

They hope the dispute will be resolved, or postponed, by greater tolerance or ideological compromise.

Such an approach is too passive. It fails to emphasize that humans have contrasting kinds of inquiry into questions about who they are, from where they came and to where they are destined. A religious inquiry relies on different presumptions and criteria than science. Because science cannot account for every question humans imagine, however, does not mean religion—disguised by some advocates as intelligent design—needs to be included in a science class. Nor does exegesis of, say, passages from Psalms or the Koran regarding proper human conduct, need discussion about the mating patterns of chimpanzees and monkeys.

Those who deride the truths of religion in the name of science undermine the value science places on curiosity. And those who demand that modern science include some mention of religion not only demean science—they do spirituality a disservice.

Goucher Unfair to Accused Professor

You preachers of equality: Your most secret ambitions to be tyrants thus shroud themselves in words of virtue. —Nietzsche

Are violations of rights relevant only in distant lands? Does the conviction that everyone is equal before the law become a fiction when possible injustice occurs in our own backyard?

This seems to be the case in light of a recent announcement that Goucher College removed a professor from his teaching duties. Leopold Munyakazi, a French teacher, has been accused of participating in genocide in his native Rwanda in 1994. While his claims of innocence are predicable, the assertions and responses surrounding his removal are remarkably surprising.

Goucher President Sanford Ungar publicly acknowledges that he lacked any evidence to prove beyond a reasonable doubt anything that "would either convict or exonerate Dr. Munyakazi." So far, there are only rumors floating on the Internet and indictments threatened by the corrupt Rwandan government. Both of these sources are notoriously unreliable for establishing any coherent legal charges, especially over something as horrible as genocide.

Unabashed by the fact that lawyers, judges and juries—not college presidents—determine guilt or innocence before the law, Mr. Ungar defended his actions with the current "words of virtue." Paramount was not justice before the law but the "best interests" of the Goucher community.

This action is not without precedent, of course. To make a much more dramatic example: Under the Bush administration, hundreds of men were held in Guatanamo Bay prison as suspected terrorists. It is not common knowledge that they were denied the basic rights every American would expect. Supposedly liberal academicians across the country's college campuses pilloried the Bush administration as an international embarrassment for punishing these suspects without any trial. Yet, when one their colleagues is suspended without any concrete evidence, the public hear a veritable conspiracy of silence.

In any event, the punishment of Dr. Munyakazi has another precedent. It appears whenever people become angry or frustrated with conventional law enforcement. This is found in vigilantism or lynching. Vigilantes are impatient. They sense that someone is getting away with a crime that only they can apprehend or punish the miscreant.

There is a chance that Mr. Munyakazi did commit a horrible deed. Maybe a prisoner in Guantanamo Bay participated in an act of terrorism. But these possibilities are to be determined after the facts are provided, not before. Hence, our legal presumption of innocent until proven guilty.

To circumvent the conventions of modern law, too many preachers of equality are not really worried about justice. Whether they are lackeys for the Bush administration or professional academics, they yearn for the power of a tyrant, shrouded with the words of virtue.

In fiction and reality, terrorists don't always fit profile

Picture a man planting a bomb that winds up killing innocent children and their mothers. The man is later videotaped shooting an unarmed suspect upon a moment's introduction. He then severs the victim's head and places it in a bowling bag for delivery to another target. His name and reputation understandably strike a mixture of fear and awe among countless enemies. Is this a known terrorist profile? Have we accurately traced the lives of al-Qaida followers or native insurgents?

In fact, this portrait draws from the resume of Jack Bauer, an erstwhile Counter Terrorism Unit (CTU) agent for the United States portrayed by Keifer Sutherland in the hit Fox series 24. Disdainful of rules and hierarchy, ever alert and daring, often in love and defiant of death, Mr. Bauer is like Indiana Jones but for one crucial element: Whereas Mr. Jones explores the source of a sacred relic, Mr. Bauer seeks the source of a terrorist plot.

Mr. Bauer's search this season has sparked considerable controversy. The series has been accused of depicting terrorists in a way that fuels barbaric stereotypes of Muslim fundamentalists. And, critics contend, the harsh tactics used by adversaries condones the use of torture. Thus, 24 risks demonizing all Muslims while legitimizing human cruelty.

These accusations are shortsighted. They fail to see how the lessons of 24 address the haphazard nature of profiling terrorists and the human element lingering amid the savagery of terror. To that extent, the show reflects the findings of scholars: When it comes to terrorism, everyone is a suspect and anyone can be a victim.

During 24's four-year run, terrorists and their accomplices have spanned the globe. Europeans and Mexicans, men and women, people with ideologies, vengeance or grandiose visions, and humans of all shades have been willing to kidnap harmless individuals, threaten unwitting populations and massacre the innocent. Even Mr. Bauer was fooled by an ex-girlfriend who turned out to be a traitor and mercilessly executed his wife.

CTU's tactics for gaining leverage also undermine the image that terrorists are simply monsters. Though they cannot be bribed or persuaded by appealing for the lives of civilians, Mr. Bauer's antagonists invariably hesitate and tremble when they discover that one of their own is held hostage. The best bargaining chip is a son or daughter. Suddenly, viewers discover that terrorists do have emotions; they are capable of deep hatred as well as intense love.

Historians remind us that the birth of terrorism is not international, but internal. Kings and tyrants brought waves of terror upon their citizens. Suspicion of heresy, guilt by association, sometimes merely being in the wrong place at the wrong time could make one the target of a ruthless despot and his bloodthirsty henchmen.

Terror terrorizes. Lacking any recognizable or conventional sense of proportion or justice, it hovers just beyond the horizon, striking with surprise and unseemly arbitrariness. The United States, in addition to aiding foreign despots, has suffered its share of terror, notably among vigilantes and antigovernment forces, whether radical or reactionary. It is no accident that books on terrorism in libraries are shelved not with history or warfare but between the sections on juvenile delinquency and gangs.

It's time to move past the slogan that one man's freedom fighter is another's terrorist. More significantly, as 24 illustrates and events confirm, anyone with enough passion, financial resources and technical knowledge is a potential terrorist: the Ku Klux Klan or the Students for a Democratic Society, Menachem Begin or Eldridge Cleaver, Eric the Red or the Capital Beltway snipers. This makes anyone a potential victim: the black, the wealthy, the colonialists, the white, the contented or the commuters, you or me.

Beatles: After 50 years, still the sound of the future

The noise they made was the sound of the future.
Even though I hadn't seen the world, I heard the
*whole world screaming. I didn't **see** it--I heard and*
felt it. —Andrew Loog Oldham, on encountering
The Beatles

Today marks the 50th anniversary of The Beatles' official United States debut, when they first appeared on the Ed Sullivan Show—the country's most-watched television program—and lit a generation on fire. By the end of 1964, John Lennon, Paul McCartney, George Harrison and Ringo Starr were international stars, cultural icons and on their way toward becoming the most profitable cash cow in the history of the music business.

Media attention to this occasion started weeks ago with music shows and magazine covers highlighting the advent of Beatlemania. Naysayers shrug off the event as just another trip down nostalgia lane for baby boomers, who commemorated the 50th anniversary of JFK's death a few months ago and are now ready to move on to the cheerier Beatles trend.

But celebrating 50 years of The Beatles shows the band was more than a passing fad; it's a testimony to their enduring appeal. Current musical groups and figures such as Arcade Fire, Flaming Lips, Gnarls Barkley and Tori Amos credit The Beatles for their own creative directions. Go to a film revival showing "Yellow Submarine," and you will find 6-year-olds joyfully jumping up and down in the seats and aisles.

Americans have a special reason to commemorate today. Each Beatle adored the range and intensity of American music—from blues and country to girl groups and early Motown. They especially worshiped the pioneers of rock and roll. For them Elvis Presley, Little Richard, Hank Williams, Roy Orbison, Carole King, Chuck Berry and Buddy Holly and The Crickets were epiphanies. In pre-fame days, The Beatles were a live juke-box of recent American music.

While learning and performing music of their masters, The Beatles themselves became masters of creating and presenting songs. However inexplicable—four kids drop out of school, ignore their parents' disapproval and become a musical and cultural event—The Beatles' revolutionary contribution to the art and popularity of the song is striking.

Consider the evidence. The Beatles set the record for the most No. 1 hits (20) and albums (15)—a Ruthian accomplishment that still stands. One week they owned the top five singles in the Billboard charts, an unimaginable feat. In the latest Rolling Stone survey of rock critics on the 500 greatest rock albums of all time, five of the top 15 are by The Beatles, with Sgt. Pepper's Lonely Hearts Club Band ranked at No. 1.

And the top selling CD of the 21st century is "1," a collection of The Beatles' No. 1 singles in the UK and U.S., which has surpassed 30 million in sales. These sales are not driven by baby boomers, who likely have these songs in duplicate on their old LPs, 45s and other compilations of their favorite group. This international market is led by younger generations having their first sustained experience of music that was so radically new in February 1964.

Songs written by The Beatles are continually covered. The first release by The Rolling Stones, "I Wanna Be Your Man," was a John Lennon-Paul McCartney ditty. "We Can Work It Out" became a Stevie Wonder hit. "Lucy in the Sky" reached No. 1 for Elton John. Siouxsie and the Banshees have a widely played version of "Dear Prudence." Rufus Wainwright's bluesy version of "Across the Universe" can be heard on radio stations. "Yesterday" is the most recorded song of all time. Add in covers by Aretha Franklin, Frank Sinatra and Elvis Presley and we have a veritable hall of fame of singers giving their renditions of the Beatles' songs. Obviously, such a legacy cannot be attributed to something so trite as boomer-nostalgia.

John, Paul, George and Ringo exemplified a very unusual human experience—a creative collaboration and friendship that marks one of the most impressive artistic events of the past century. Through this musical friendship they brought their own creative craft of writing and recording songs about teenage love, childhood memories, moments of joy and death, desire and despair. They told stories of loneliness and self-doubt—three- to four-minute perspectives on the human experience.

To focus on one's own memories between 1964 and 1970, when the band broke up, might be boomer-nostalgia. But when younger generations study, play and dance to Beatles' music, then to celebrate their 50th anniversary is not just about the past. It is to respect—and even love—the Beatle sound that still thrives today and will endure into the future.

When & Where

About the Author

Alexander E. Hooke is a Baltimore native, and has lived in the city for over fifty years. He and his two children have attended public schools and enjoyed the range of experiences in urban life, though also aware of its drawbacks. He attended the Community College of Baltimore, Towson State, and University of Missouri, and has taught at Villa Julie College/Stevenson University since 1978. He has published *Virtuous Persons, Vicious Deeds* and *Encounters with Alphonso Lingis*, in addition to numerous academic articles.

Apprentice
House Press
Loyola University Maryland

Apprentice House is the country's only campus-based, student-staffed book publishing company. Directed by professors and industry professionals, it is a nonprofit activity of the Communication Department at Loyola University Maryland.

Using state-of-the-art technology and an experiential learning model of education, Apprentice House publishes books in untraditional ways. This dual responsibility as publishers and educators creates an unprecedented collaborative environment among faculty and students, while teaching tomorrow's editors, designers, and marketers.

Outside of class, progress on book projects is carried forth by the AH Book Publishing Club, a co-curricular campus organization supported by Loyola University Maryland's Office of Student Activities.

Eclectic and provocative, Apprentice House titles intend to entertain as well as spark dialogue on a variety of topics. Financial contributions to sustain the press's work are welcomed. Contributions are tax deductible to the fullest extent allowed by the IRS.

To learn more about Apprentice House books or to obtain submission guidelines, please visit www.apprenticehouse.com.

Apprentice House
Communication Department
Loyola University Maryland
4501 N. Charles Street
Baltimore, MD 21210
Ph: 410-617-5265 • Fax: 410-617-2198
info@apprenticehouse.com • www.apprenticehouse.com